The Mentor-Disciple Relationship in the Visual Arts and Beyond

I0473368

This book undertakes a deep examination of mentor and disciple relationships in the development of artists. It draws upon a variety of relationships and models, including an in-person mentor, a mentor or apprentice scenario, and non-physical mentors such as historical figures, in order to investigate their history and philosophy.

This volume specifically addresses the role of mentoring in the lives of contemporary aspiring artists, asking if and how mentoring can be considered a form of human nurturance. Deep historical inspections and philosophical inquiries are combined with analyses of interviews with contemporary artists ranging from 35 to 101 years old. These holistic insights present the subject of mentoring in the arts from the multiple angles of art history and relevant ideas about the benefits of nurturance and acceptance in human development.

Using artists' biographies and discussions of their work, this book sheds light on the role that mentoring has played in their development and can play in contemporary education. It will appeal to artists, art history teachers, educators, art students, and art scholars.

Gaetano A. LaRoche is an artist and teacher at an elementary school in NYC. He holds an Ed.D. in Art and Art Education from Columbia University Teachers College, NYC.

Routledge Research in Arts Education

The Mentor-Disciple Relationship in the Visual Arts and Beyond

Mentoring as Human Nurturing

Gaetano A. LaRoche

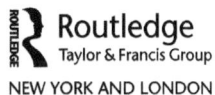

Routledge
Taylor & Francis Group

NEW YORK AND LONDON

First published 2025
by Routledge
605 Third Avenue, New York, NY 10158

and by Routledge
4 Park Square, Milton Park, Abingdon, Oxon, OX14 4RN

Routledge is an imprint of the Taylor & Francis Group, an informa business

ISBN: 9781032586632 (hbk)
ISBN: 9781032587400 (pbk)
ISBN: 9781003451303 (ebk)

DOI: 10.4324/9781003451303

Typeset in Times New Roman
by KnowledgeWorks Global Ltd.

For Anya and Sophia.

Contents

1 Introduction

In this chapter, I discuss the term mentor, where it came from, as well as from where my interest in the subject derives. I present the arts as an area of discipline and disciplines as areas that need masters and disciples, and mentors and disciples.

This book is about life and the nurturance of life through caring, teaching, and mentorship. It focuses on the visual art as that is my background and strongest interest. Looking at human nurturance through mentoring, caring for others in the visual arts also includes looking at copying as a way of discipleship and learning, copying not just products, but ways of thinking, being, and valuing.

Mentor, the man that Odysseus charged with raising and caring for his son Telemachus while he went off to fight in the Trojan War, took on the full charge of a father to nurture Telemachus and teach him what he needed to know to grow into manhood. This Greek figure from which the term, the noun, and the verb to mentor come from took on the responsibilities of fatherhood for another's son. It is important to keep in mind the level of responsibility that comes from the term mentor. It is not a two-week or one-year term. Mentor cared for Telemachus for nearly two decades.

Just as Virgil led Dante through the rings of hell in *The Inferno*, so too does an aspiring artist's mentor who lead him through the trials of being an artist. The artist's mentor, like Virgil and Mentor, seeks to guide, enlighten, protect, challenge, and nourish.

Through enlightenment in the field of being an artist, a mentor may nourish the young aspiring artist's interest that brought him to the mentor. A mentor may inform the younger person of ways of making, mixing material, seeing, and conceptualizing ideas to forms and forms themselves. A good mentor, as all mentors are by definition, cares for two things passionately: for the art being transmitted, the information or field of his life's work; and for the disciple. Without both, there can be no mentor and disciple relationship, no mentoring or transmission of values from one generation to the next, thus ensuring the continuation and growth of the discipline and the ones who make and do the work of the discipline—the disciples.

DOI: 10.4324/9781003451303-1

Disciples are not just disciples of the mentor. They first want to be disciples of the discipline. In this book, the discipline is the field of art making. Many are the disciplines to which people have trained their thoughts and labors. All are of worth—hence the very reason people put their energies into them. Moreover, all have aspirants and masters. My discipline has been painting and drawing and those forms that spring from them. My interests include sculpture, architecture, installations, literature, film, and photography; all are visual, some more tactile than others, some flickering lights, some pigment on a surface, and some forms holding weight and changing lived space.

Here, I will discuss the role of mentoring in the development of the next generation of artists. I will consider the dynamics of the mentor and disciple relationship from a historical perspective of predominately Western European artists' training and from interviews with four contemporary artists. Here in this text, disciple will mean one who willingly and knowingly goes to another to learn with great devotion.

I will discuss how the mentor and disciple came to know each other, how they came to trust and play the roles they chose. Here, I choose to work with Sartre's (2001) belief that everything we do is a choice, for even if it is a choice between death and dishonor, it is a choice. Just as it is a choice to mentor or ignore, it is a choice. So too, one chooses to receive over to refuse; to receive a person as a mentor or refuse them; to seek wisdom in the words of the elder or to reject them as a fool—each is a choosing of the other.

The Problem

Background to the Problem

We all grow through others, through our interactions with them. As social creatures, I believe that anything that is not biologically driven is learned through the imitation of others or their works and experimentation in movements, thoughts, and processes.

In reading interviews and writings of artists and their biographies, and in listening to what they speak about—be it in person, in their home or studio, as a member of an audience to whom they are speaking, or as a viewer of a recorded interview with another, I have found that they almost always speak of those who have influenced them and their development and continuation as artists. As an artist and teacher of art to young children, teens, and college students, I consider my influence on others and the influence of others on me. I consider these influences formative and necessary, not negative as it is sometimes portrayed in the writing and thoughts of some.

Throughout history, artists have learned their craft, their discipline, through discipleship to either a person, a group of people, or an ideal. Yet, in cultures which place great value upon the successes of the individual, that person's ability to break with tradition frequently feels like a powerful undercurrent of denying the influence, as if each person should come from nothing and no one, and yet be something miraculous and someone of marvel. I feel that this leads to a dualism of confusion for a young person caring to enter the discipline. The mixed message of "Be great!" and "Don't copy!" leaves students of the visual arts perplexed, confused, and unhappy.

A large goal of this book is to show that artists do have influences and that artists of great caliber honor their teachers and always admit to their influence. Through a historical investigation of how artists have learned their craft and grown in their discipline and through personal interviews with four contemporary artists, I hope to show that the way to making a contribution to the field of art is to enter into it humbly, seeking understanding, knowledge, skill, and growth through those who attracted one to the field of art initially.

Problem Statement

Here is the problem. Society tells its populace that to be great, one must be "new," "original," a "genius." Yet throughout human history, people have learned what is most important to them from their predecessors. Moreover, it seems that almost all learning involves the conscious or unconscious modeling of one's actions on those of another, on those whom one has seen and wants to copy, to be like or do like.

The problem extends to the development of artists in that one must ask: How can one convince students that they should study the masters, develop relationships with older artists, develop their perceptual abilities by drawing from observation, and go to museums and seek out the great works, when what they hear from the larger society is that they better be "new" if they want to succeed? Easily, a young person may become confused if not conflicted in how to proceed and in what to invest her energies: making new or listening to the old?

Because so many great artists throughout history frequently trace their greatness to another, a problem also arises that can be phrased in a couple of questions: How does one find a mentor? Given that mentors do play a significant role in the development and continued work of artists, how are they to be found? The author sought to gain insight into how mentors have contributed to the formation of thinking processes, beliefs, and working methods of artists, and how it is that the mentor and disciple relationship commenced and sustained itself over time by interviewing four artists about the mentors in their lives. This author also sought to find out if copying played a role in the artists' development or in their relationships with their mentors.

In this book, mentors are those chosen by artists to model themselves on. These include people they have worked with in the same time and place, as well as those from the history of their discipline, to whom I here refer as mentors in the mind.

Theoretical Problem Statement

There is no definition of the mentor and disciple role in today's structured education of artists. I here want to argue against the prevailing notion that artists do not need mentors and should not seek to model themselves on one. I argue that not only due to the rapidly expanding forms that constitute art but also *because* of this very phenomenon, aspiring artists need direction and guidance more than ever to avoid getting lost in the many, many options available for expressing forms and ideas and media to choose from and work in, all in the name of being an artist.

Art = the physical, tangible.

Ideas = thoughts.

Great art = thoughts or movement or some valued aspect of intangible life made tangible, such as light caught in a painting, movement caught in a drawing, and history captured in a photograph.

Artist = one who gives tangible form to the vision.

Vision = a particular artist's way of seeing the world, life, and experience.

Cultural Problem Statement

With the explosion of accepted forms of presenting ideas in the arts that include anything from making marks on paper (drawing); to speaking and moving in person to an audience (performance); to changing a space to make it into something else (installation); to expressing ideas, interests, and points of view via flickering light (video); to documenting the manipulation of one's body (body art); to so many other yet-to-be-tried and accepted forms and modes, the person entering the field of art has so much to choose from that it is, as with so many things presented by God and society, both a blessing and a burden.

Educational Problem Statement

Given what can be gained from a combination of historical research and interview research in the subject of mentor and disciple relationships in the development of artists, it is hoped that such new and not so new but newly-looked-upon knowledge will provide insights to teachers about the roles and ways they may affect their students and present options for relating beyond what is current popular pedagogy and popular meaning, merely that which is used most by the populace. The populace in this case are the teachers and students in the development of artists for this society.

Reference

Sartre, J. P. (2001). *Jean-Paul Sartre: Basic writings* (S. Priest ed.). New York, NY: Routledge.

2 Characteristics of Mentors

In this chapter, I discuss the essential characteristics of mentors and how a mentor is different than a teacher. I consider mentoring in relation to the sustaining and continuing of a craft or discipline and how it involves issues of parenting, caring and nurturance.

Elements of Mentorships

Hospitality

Hospitality, Snowber (2005) notes, is one of the key elements in the mentoring relationship. The mentor graciously receives the disciple into his home or workspace, accepting him and offering all that he has. I have been the recipient of such generosity at the academy of capoeira Mestre João Grande. He has fed me, provided me a home to go to and be with others, accepted me time and time again when I did not accept myself, and made clear to others that I was to be honored, accepted. This did not happen in the first class, nor during the first year, nor even the second. Yet over time as Mestre Grande saw more and more of me and my care for capoeira and growth and efforts therein, he invited me more and more to come closer as he saw my desire was to do so.

My experience of gradually going from an unknown to a known student of Mestre João Grande, and of others who have cared for me to my great fortune, relate directly to Daloz's (1999) description of the mentor and disciple relationship as a journey where each takes care of and nurtures the other. As the scholars in the field of adult education Merriam, Caffarella, and Baumgartner (2007) assert, "The relationship is reciprocal and nurturing of both" (p. 205).

It Is a Relationship

O'Neil and Marsick (2009), in their summary of how mentoring has been seen traditionally, cite two kinds of relationships. One is where the purpose of the relationship is centered on the preparation of the disciple to enter the

DOI: 10.4324/9781003451303-2

chosen "career." This kind of mentoring focuses on what the career demands and the preparation for it. They then note another kind of mentor and disciple relationship which is "both intense and caring" (p. 19). It involves concern beyond the specifics of the career to include the overall well-being of the two.

Staikidis (2006) spent time in the homes and studios of artists in Guatemala. She studied painting in the studios of two Mayan artists by entering into an apprenticeship with them to learn both about painting and Mayan pedagogy. She speaks of the essential need for a relationship when learning to paint within the Mayan artistic tradition, stating that for the Mayan,

> The mentoring relationship is at the core of teaching practice. Relationships between mother and child and father and son and among siblings and teachers and students are the primary shapers in all fields of Mayan education. For the cultural outsider, the first objective within the mentoring pairs is to establish friendship and trust as the foundations for teaching and learning. (p. 125)

Just as Staikidis found that relationships between mentor and student formed the foundation for the mentoring experience in Mayan culture, Ardalan (2009) found that in the ancient transmission of craftarts skill and understanding in Iran, social engagement was paramount. Through speaking with both the mentors and their apprentices and observing them as a participant observer, she noted,

> that the creative and cognitive process of learning in a mentorship and apprenticeship setting involves the whole person in an environment of social engagements that provides the grounds for significant learning to take place. (p. ii)

Snowber (2005) emphasizes the importance of listening in the mentoring process, stating that "as human beings in a fast-paced culture, we are not necessarily trained in the art of deep or attentive listening" (p. 347). Such is the state that the disciple may not even know that the sound he is making is a yearning for knowledge and growth. The disciple listens closely for the subtle and not always so subtle instruction and wisdom of experience that the mentor holds and shares.

Haywood Rolling (2009) poetically speaks of the lasting influence of his doctoral study mentor, Graeme Sullivan. He writes:

> And he still reaches us, not to pluck any of those he has mentored as his own personal bouquet, but to run his fingers across the petals we have flowered, allowing us to seed the fields we have settled in and generate our own reincarnations. (p. 45)

Green, Mitchell, and Taylor (2011) found in the research articles they referenced that "the most important results of mentoring include security, stronger determination toward success and strengthening of self-efficacy" (p. 124). I would contend that the mentor acts like a parent in the psychological model of a securely attached child. Here, the child who believes, through what experience has shown her, that the parent is always there for her will have the confidence to explore the world and interact with others; return to the parent for reassurance, nurturance, and comfort; and go out again. The mentor for the disciple provides that source, that well of confidence, from which to go over and over again to drink, and then to go into the larger world with one's gifts and share them.

In studying mentoring among scientists and engineers, Maughan (2006) found that the quality of the relationships had a profound impact on whether the apprentice found the experience to be positive and thus career-affirming. He writes, "It is clear that the relationship between the mentor and protégé is a significant part of the entire learning experience" (p. 116). Through relationships, learning occurs.

Mentors and Disciple Are Family

Learning requires growth and change, change of conceptions or behaviors, and this in itself can cause unease and anxiety. Even if the anxiety is not clearly expressed, it is a great impediment to growth and learning. Here, Ardalan (2009) describes what Ostaad Pashai, an Iranian potter in Tehran, believed about the necessity for the mentor to know the student as a family member and an equal, and extract stress and anxiety from them. She writes,

> Ostaad Pashai believed that the master had to find the anxieties of the students and that each student differed from one to another; he believed that the teacher/mentor had to work with the student as an equal, as a family, and pull out of them any stress and anxiety they might have. (p. 110)

In Albert Camus' last work, *The First Man*, published posthumously decades after his death by his daughter, he speaks of the role that others play as parents who are not; who are not the parent of the person being guided and cared for. Camus' (1995) autobiographical novel tells of how a teacher changed the life path of a boy by using "all his weight as a man to change" the possibilities for the child.

> This man had never known his father, but he often spoke to Jacques of him in a rather mythological way, and in any case at a critical time he knew how to take the father's role. That is why Jacques had never forgotten him, as if, having never really felt the lack of a father he had never known, he

had nonetheless subconsciously recognized, first as a child, then during the rest of his life, the one paternal act-both well thought out and crucial-that had affected his life as a child. For M. Bernard, his teacher for the year of the *certificate d'etudes*, had at a given moment used all his weight as a man to change the destiny of this child in his charge, and he had in fact changed it. (p. 137)

An Opportunity to Guide Students

What began as a pragmatic necessity developed into a lifelong passion. Teaching fulfilled him; it provided him with a forum for presenting his ideas and an opportunity to guide students.

(Dreishpoon, 2002, p. 29)

The above quote about the American artist Edwin Dickenson speaks of how he began teaching as a means of livelihood as sales of paintings did not provide for him and his family and how from this necessity to provide came a "passion for teaching." There is a long history of artists teaching. Of the New York School artists, Arshile Gorky, Mark Rothko, Philip Guston, and Hans Hofmann all taught art to people in a range of ages and a range of settings (Anfam, 1990).

The Mentor as Expert

In the *Inferno*, Dante's "Virgil remains expert on the much more familiar terrain that the pilgrim must traverse" (Freccero, 1994, p. xvi). The designation or quality of expert is as necessary to being a guide as wings are necessary to being a bird. To continue the analogy of wings and birds, for a bird to take flight, it must have two healthy wings. And so, a mentor must also have the two wings of caring and expertise.

Mentors Care

Perhaps those are crucial aspects of one who becomes a mentor—concern and caring for another—usually beginning with the older person seeking to guide a younger one and almost always the younger one developing deep concern, love, and affection for the older one who expresses in word and deed consistent concern for the well-being and aspirations of the younger. Daloz (1999) writes, "What makes the difference is their willingness to care about what they teach and whom" (p. 20).

By caring, one demonstrates goodness, even without the intention of doing so, and this is not lost upon the apprentice who, although young, is not foolish enough to trust someone who does not have goodness within. I would say from reflection on my experiences of being mentored and on the words of those who believe I mentored them that two qualities must be present in a mentor. She must be both qualified and caring or caring and qualified. Qualified means this person can show me some of the path to being as artist because she also has walked that path and achieved the title of artist in the minds of others. Caring means that I feel cared for, looked out for.

From the quotes of my interviews that appear later in this book, one will see that Will Barnet cared about painting, drawing, printmaking, and studying the great works of the past, but that he cared more for people. He knew that he was an expert, well-versed in the history of art and skill of art making, and this is what he had to share with others. The concern that a student absorbs becomes the guiding force in life. Will Barnet cared dearly for those who cared about painting, drawing, and printmaking and came before him as students. Through the instance of learning came relationships that continued for 50 years and more.

One will also consider if Jarrod Beck's mentor, Javier, cared more about architecture, or about the young man Jarrod who expressed interest and showed passion. Caring for others is caring for oneself, I argue. In nurturing Jarrod, was Javier nurturing his younger self? Was Jarrod presenting Javier with a chance to go back and care for Javier, the Javier he was when he was 20? Was Jarrod, in tending to Javier, tending to a father figure who was hardly present in his own upbringing, a father figure with shared interests and a lifestyle he desired?

Masters Must Be Alone

Steiner (2003) argues that in the end, the master must be alone. For a master to be such, he must have much time alone to be with his craft, thought, and philosophy. Time is needed for the master to grow. In Steiner's look at the behaviors of masters in many fields, including philosophy, literature, and music, he describes an archetype that emerges:

> The archetype of the Master is that of a sage who withdraws into and then descends from the high places. His teaching gathers to it disciples, but will incite them to abandon him. (p. 114)

Steiner speaks of Nietzsche and writes of how his thoughts made it necessary for him to be alone. Perhaps this was first, so that he could form them and second, because others would not understand them. Thus, the time alone was a time of formation—a formation of what would attract disciples later.

But, without others to impart the knowledge, wisdom, or insight gained, the master is naught. There can be no master or mentor without others to recognize this, that this person has mastered something profound, and so we seek to be near him or her to learn this or that thing. Steiner speaks of the need for both solitude and communion when he writes, "Without solitude there is no vision; without an audience, however restricted, no truths can be revealed" (p. 117).

Craft as Learning Process and Cultural Transmission

On the surface, one learns some things to be able to do that thing. While this is true, it is not all. One learns to draw to learn to draw, and in doing so increases one's perception of the world and likely one's appreciation of it and humility before it. One learns capoeira to play capoeira, and this is true. But one also learns to be with others, be comfortable with oneself, feel the movement of energy, value life. Every teacher teaches many things. While teaching drawing, I am also teaching the value of quiet and looking, concentrating, respecting others' need for the same and the value of looking at the light.

Ardalan (2009) studied four masters of craftart in contemporary Iran and came to believe that "The craftart that they made was seen less as independent objects and more as a process through which they passed down their knowledge to apprentices" (p. 79). The masters were not so interested in the making of objects as they were in transmitting knowledge and beliefs to the next generation. As she studied the master craftsmen and their apprentices, she reflected on the centuries of transmission of craft knowledge and skill through the mentor and apprentice tradition in Iran. She cited the work of Fiouzat (1993) when stating that the responsibility for preserving the ancient crafts through training the next generation was that of the village elders and family members. She writes that the apprenticeship

> was communal and experience-based as apprentices sat next to a mentor and learned by watching and by doing. The mentor was a parent, a grandparent, an uncle or aunt, or acquaintance and the apprentice lived and worked with them from an early age, usually seven. (p. 49)

The Place of Words Spoken

When the master speaks, the words alone do not carry the learning. And the subject, often not of the methods or ways of the discipline directly, may be about anything. It is from this speaking and the disciple listening that insights are given and gained. There is the metaphorical speaking. There is the allegorical speaking. And then there is just the master speaking about what he cares about in a way that transmits to the disciple what is of value or not to him; from that, the disciple considers the why and comes more to understand the master, his reasons and goals.

When Capoeira Mestre João Grande tells a group of students, "There are no big men here. The only big people are Jasmine and Zacky," it is understood by all present that he is saying multiple things of great import. First, that while some capoeira students appear "big" or have great strengths, Mestre does not think so. Everyone is a student. Second, Jasmine and Zacky were children about 3 and 6 years of age when he said this. He was saying to the students, "You are no different to me than little children." Most importantly, Mestre Grande was saying to the group—as affirmed in many of his other words and behaviors—that what he values the most is children and, specifically here, his grandchildren, for they are the "big people here."

In this book, as in my life as an artist, and in the discussion of the historical mentorship of Arshile Gorky (Rosenberg, 1962; Schwabacher, 1957), I argue for the role that artists of the past can play continually in the growth and work of an artist. I call them mentors in our minds, as we have never met them, yet still they guide us. And, when speaking with Will Barnet for this study, he affirmed this belief in his own life's work. Yet at the same time, just as it can be cold and sunny at the same time, in being with a master side by side in the same room hearing him speak and watching the reactions of the master to others and events, one learns things that would otherwise not be learned.

Steiner (2003), in considering the *Lessons of the Masters*, asserts that orality is a central component in the learning relationship. The master speaks to the student, and the student asks questions and speaks to the master of her concerns, aspirations, and life. Steiner writes,

> Before writing, during the history of writing and in challenge to it, the spoken word is integral to the act of teaching. The master speaks to the disciple. From Plato to Wittgenstein, the ideal of lived truth is one of orality, of face to face address and response. (p. 8)

How a Teacher Is Different From a Mentor

A teacher is for the many. A mentor is for the few. I had many fine teachers at The Cooper Union. During my four years there, with one in Paris, I would say I had only one mentor, Nicholas Marsicano. Henry Finkelstein said much the same thing: "They were fine teachers ..." but Kadish and Marsicano were different.

A teacher teaches everyone in the class. A mentor takes in a few, as it would not be possible to do more. Teachers are crucial, necessary. They teach subjects, knowledge gleaned already by others and recorded, and ways of doing, thinking about, and making things. Mentors guide. They give direction, not solely skill or even knowledge. Through time spent listening to them side by side in their presence, one may develop knowledge of the discipline, of self, of possibilities in this time called life. I would say they do not even teach subjects or content, but rather they teach individuals about themselves and their possibilities in a discipline through the content of the discipline, sometimes and sometimes not. What they are really teaching—and this is why they are frequently older than most—is about life.

Yes, as a painting professor or sculpture professor, one may care passionately about these arts and the ones connected with and influenced by them. But what makes a man a mentor is his care for another, his emotional investment in the welfare and future of another because he loves. He loves life, and there is life in the young. Life as a journey is tricky and so the one who loves life seeks to guide, reassure, and strengthen for the long journey the ones willing to apprentice, listen, and attend, and be a fellow on the journey of living. And this lasts until one passes the baton to the other or at least until one is sure that the younger cares and has force enough to grab the baton.

Mentoring and Adult Education

Adult education differs in substantial ways from elementary and secondary school education and even from college when students go there directly after completing high school (Merriam et al., 2007). In numerous ways, the mentoring process occurs in adult education sites and situations.

Because many in adult education are more self-directed and mature, they can pursue their needs with greater clarity than younger students who may be in school only because they believe that is what people their age do in this society. One of the aspects of the mentor and student relationship is that the student is in need of direction and so seeks out a mentor, whether consciously or less so.

When Mezirow (1981) talks about "perspective transformation in human development" (p. 3), that is very much what happens during the mentor and disciple relationship as the disciple comes increasingly to see the world and the art he is studying in new ways and perspectives.

One of the characteristics of adult learners (Merriam et al., 2007) is that they are seeking change in their lives. That is often the reason they have returned to schooling of some kind, even though they may be married, with children, and employed—all hallmarks of adulthood in every society. In seeking change, adults seek not only places, but people in those places who can guide them from where they are professionally and personally to another place they aspire to be.

Illeris (2007) names energy as one of the necessary elements of learning in his theory because learning is not passive. To learn, one must expend energy in thought and doing. This choice is more conscious in adult learners because not only do they have greater ability to choose to be in the learning situation or not. But they likely have far greater responsibilities for themselves and others so the choice to spend one's time and energy to learn something from another usually comes with the understanding that one is also choosing to expend energy toward a goal.

Mezirow (1981) identifies three domains of learning:

> Each of three distinct but interrelated domains-controlling and manipulating the environment, social interaction and perspective transformation-involves different ways of knowing and hence different learning needs, different educational and methods and different of research and evaluation. (p. 21)

These are all a part of a disciple's training. "Manipulating the environment" for an artist means taking physical materials, the environment, and shaping them, manipulating them to create something that was not there before: a chair, a painting, an installation, a video, or a bowl.

Successful "social interaction" is necessary to participate in any discipline, for without others, there is no appreciation for one's efforts, no challenges posed, and no one with whom to share one's successes and failings. Successful social interaction as an artist allows one to present work to others, who in turn may create or know of opportunities for reaching audiences that an artist cannot reach in isolation. It also allows for the happiness and pleasure that can come from interacting with others in discussing ideas, working together to present work or create work, hearing another's voice.

The role of "perspective transformation" as a master works with a disciple is to make clear the many, and to emphasize the most salient, ways of seeing the discipline and the participants in the field of the discipline. Does an artist aspire to "make work for Soho or for the Louvre"? Thus Ruben Kadish challenged his students at The Cooper Union at a time when Soho was an area of Manhattan where new galleries were popping up every other day and work was being sold, work that he believed was mostly shallow, not like the work in the Lourve.

In the above example, if a young person has the perspective that the goal of being an artist is to have exhibitions in the currently popular and populated gallery system, and to become popular there and sell work to the people who visit its boutiques and galleries, then Kadish was seeking with his words to transform perspectives and pose the challenge to his students to create work that would last beyond current popularity and have qualities that would sustain its appreciation over centuries.

References

Anfam, D. (1990). *Abstract expressionism*. London, UK: Thames and Hudson.

Ardalan, S. (2009). *Apprenticeship in the arts and crafts of Iran: The mentorship practices of four masters*. Unpublished dissertation, EdD, Teachers College, Columbia University, New York, NY.

Camus, A. (1995). *The first man*. New York, NY: Alfred A. Knopf.

Daloz, L. A. (1999). *Mentor: Guiding the journey of adult learners* (2nd ed.). San Francisco, CA: Jossey-Bass.

Dreishpoon, D. (2002). *Edwin Dickenson: Dreams and realities.* New York, NY: Hudson Hills Press.

Fiouzat, E. (1993). *Baresiyeh Tahavolateh Nezameh Ostaad Shagerdi dar Iran (A look at the changes of the practices of mentorship/apprenticeship in Iran).* Tehran, Iran: Shahid Beheshti University Press.

Freccero, J. (1994). Foreword. In Dante (Ed.), *Inferno* (R. Pinsky, trans.). New York, NY: Noonday Press.

Green, D., Mitchell, T. & Taylor, P. (2011). Mentoring in the art classroom. *Improving Schools. 14*(2), 117–129.

Haywood Rolling, J. Jr. (2009). Carnations and reincarnations in open fields of play. In A. Kantawala, L. Hochtritt, J. Haywood Rolling, D. Serig, & K. Stakidis (Eds.), Establishing collaborative dialogue: The mentor and the apprentice. *Visual Arts Research, 35*(2), 40–50.

Illeris, K. (2007). *How we learn: Learning and non-learning in school and beyond.* London, UK: Routledge.

Maughan, B. D. (2006). *Mentoring among scientists: Implications of interpersonal relationships within a formal mentoring program.* Albuquerque, NM: Winter Meeting and Nuclear Technology Expo.

Merriam, S. B., Caffarella, R. S., & Baumgartner, L. M. (2007). *Learning in adulthood: A comprehensive guide* (3rd ed.). San Francisco, CA: Jossey-Bass.

Mezirow, J. (1981). A critical theory of adult learning and education. *Adult Education Quarterly, 32*(3), 3–24.

O'Neil, J., & Marsick, V. (2009). Peer mentoring and action learning. *Adult Learning, 20*(1–2), 19–24.

Rosenberg, H. (1962). *Arshile Gorky: The man, the time, the idea.* New York, NY: The Sheep Meadow Press/Flying Point Books.

Schwabacher, E. K. (1957). *Arshile Gorky.* New York, NY: Macmillan.

Snowber, C. (2005). The mentor as artist: A poetic exploration of listening, creating, and mentoring. *Mentoring & Tutoring, 13*(3), 345–353.

Staikidis, K. (2006). Personal and cultural narrative as inspiration: A painting and pedagogical collaboration with Mayan artists. *Studies in Art Education, 47*(2), 118–138.

Steiner, G. (2003). *Lessons of the masters.* Cambridge, MA: Harvard University Press.

3 Copying as a Way of Discipleship

Introduction

In this chapter, I consider copying as one way of learning and discipleship. I discuss artists who have copied the works of other artists and consider the reasons why they did so. I look at the historical uses of copying by artists, seek to define the many kinds of copying, discuss philosophical and pedagogical considerations for doing so or not, and discuss my use of copying to develop as an artist.

> In general, the copy has been made with the most honest intentions to fulfill a need, engendered in Hellenistic times if not earlier, which persons have had for more than one version of an image. But if this has been the main cause for making copies, it has not been the only one.
>
> (Ayrton, 1960, p. 8)

In copying the works of an admired artist, one may be seeking to learn from them, learn how to make paintings or sculptures like the admired master. I argue that it is a way of discipleship, a way of learning with a long, long history, and one way taken up by many a great artist.

Some Philosophical Discussion

When Dore Ashton (1980) writes in *A Fable of Modern Art*, "He [Cézanne] said he would do Poussin after nature. In the end, he did Poussin after his *own* nature" (p. 46), she identifies the phenomenon I seek to consider: how one, an artist in this case, can model himself after another, yet in the end, it is his own nature that comes through. It is his energy creating the new with the model of the old in sight.

I agree with Sartre (1962) when he writes about Albert Camus' take on life: "And besides, everything has the same value, whether it be writing *The Possessed* or drinking a cup of coffee" (p. 112). Whether one makes a painting of a person or a painting of a painting, it would seem to have the same

DOI: 10.4324/9781003451303-3

value—pigment on a surface arranged by a person to convey some thought on something now looked at by another person who is trying to decipher or gain insight or pleasure from the looking.

Hughes (2006), in his doctoral dissertation *The Moral Nature of Artistic Genius*, argues that it is the willing submission of artists to tradition, and hence their forbearers, that allows both for the continuation of the discipline and for innovation therein. The originality paradox that McFarland (1985) defines in *Originality and Imagination* is the need to be new, original, and so different from one's predecessors and to grow from the tradition that is so rich, and because of its richness which attracted the artist in the first place, it plays out continually. Sometimes the emphasis of the society which is situated in a specific time is on affording great reverence to the past, while during other centuries, the dominant trend has been on an insistence on the new. McFarland traces the originality paradox throughout history, from Plato to Emerson and Classicism to Romanticism. He sees the struggle between staying home and going away, between seeking the tradition to breaking away and making new the tradition, played out over and over in each generation.

Yet, "It is also clear that if there be *no* self-expression, no free play of individuality, the product will of necessity be but an instance of a species" (Dewey, 1936, p. 107), and therein lies the paradox. How does the artist train to be like his predecessors and still make a contribution of his own? The solution can be in what Pan (2007) sees in the Eastern tradition of entering into the master's craft and mindset so as to form, develop one's self. Yet always, and in the end, one is one's self, and so the master will shine anew through the student. In the long European tradition of apprenticeship, it is expected, even known, that the student will grow into his own and that his time as an apprentice is for the very purpose of making the artist, craft person, anew.

Learning the Language

Before one can speak of the inconsistencies of the language, one must learn it. By this I mean that before one can create new words or phrases, or before they can be identified as new by others hearing or reading them, one must know the language being built upon. So it is with art. Art cannot be new unless it is compared to what is and was, and so is now considered old.

> Just as in writing we learn a particular basic form of letters and then vary it later, so we learn first the stability of things as the norm, which is then subject to alterations.
>
> (Wittgenstein, 1972, p. 62)

The "stability" of art must be learned for one to make "alterations" of value. Studying the past works of art and copying them as part of the study contributes to the learning of the "norm" from which future work will spring.

The great American artist Romare Bearden, who became most known for his collages depicting urban and rural scenes of people engaged in eating, singing, and lovemaking, "devoted about a year to copying works of art by both the old and the modern masters" (Kennel, 2003, p. 143). Though he had already achieved some success in the New York gallery world, Bearden directed his energies to the copying of the great works of history to learn the language of his chosen profession. Kennel wonderfully pairs some of Bearden's work with the paintings from which they sprang, sources as rich as the paintings of Giotto, Agnolo Bronzino, Lucas Cranach the Elder, Duccio di Buoninsegna, Dirk Bouts, and Edgar Degas among them. Kennel quotes from Bearden's own journal:

Delacroix almost to the end of his life was always going to the Louvre and copying paintings... I took perhaps two years and made a very systematic study of the Old Masters... (p. 143)

Two years of copying may seem like a long time to some. But it served Bearden well just as the copying of great works by Arshile Gorky for many years (Ashton, 1995) served him, and we who have the benefit of enjoying the fruits of their study and labor benefit immensely.

The art educator Seymour Simmons III (2008), in discussing the myths that surround notions of creativity, argues that copying has received a bad rap in our culture. He urges us to look to the East where respect for the value of learning through imitation holds its place. He also makes the connection that copying the master in this manner is a kind of preparation that allows an artist to be receptive and prepared for the moment of inspiration and execution, combining both copying with meditation as ways of training. As he writes:

the West has something to learn from the East. There, practitioners of traditional Asian arts spend years preparing themselves by copying and following precisely the directions of their masters, while simultaneously practicing meditation techniques to help them remain receptive to inspiration. (p. 58)

Does A Influence B? Or Does B Change Our Perception of A?

The complex ways in which art acts upon predecessors suggests that it is not so much the present but rather the past which is conditioned by a perpetual flux.

(van Alphen, 2004, p. 57)

The assumption that the person who copies the work of another is influenced by that person in a one-directional manner has been challenged by Baxandall (1985) in his book *Patterns of Intention* and by the cultural analyst

Mieke Bal (1999) in her book *Quoting Caravaggio: Contemporary Art, Pre-posterous History*. They ask that we consider that in the act of copying, the copier draws attention to the copied artist in a new way, resulting in new ways of seeing the copied artist and her work. The attention given by the copying artist through the act of painting anew the older artist's work changes the perception of the artist and her work. Though the artist is long dead, the new attention brings her back to the fore. The work is as new as the first day it was seen, with the copying artist's work as a lens.

Ernst van Alphen (2004) in his discussion of Francis Bacon's act of "reinventing his models" considers not only Baxandall and Bal's argument for the dual nature of influence, and its ability to change both the looker and the looked at, but he brings the argument back to T.S. Eliot, who asked long ago that we consider how the past is changed by the looking of the present. Paintings, like poems for Eliot, do not stand still. They live only when viewed in the eyes and mind of the viewer viewing; and as that always changes from century to century, so too does the painting. Just by looking, we change what is looked at, they argue.

Goodman (1976) in *Languages of Art* speaks of how the eye and mind see things based upon their need rather than solely upon what they physically perceive: "Not only how but what it sees is regulated by need and prejudice" (p. 7). When Picasso copies the paintings of Manet or when Bacon begins a painting based upon looking, studying, that of Velázquez's *Pope Innocent X*, how much of what the artist sees is based upon "need"? How much "preju-dice" occurs in the process?

"Reception and interpretation are not separable operations" (p. 8), Good-man states. He continues:

> It does not so much mirror as take and make; and what it takes and makes it sees not bare, as items without attributes, but as things, as food, as people, as enemies, as stars, as weapons. Nothing is seen nakedly or naked. (p. 8)

Like Gombrich (1956), Goodman contends that there is no such thing as image formation without prior visual experience. He refers to Kant, stating that "the innocent eye is blind" (p. 8).

The Anxiety of Copying, Not Being Original, New

> The history of fruitful poetic influence, which is to say the main tradition of Western poetry since the Renaissance, is a history of anxiety and self-saving caricature, of distortion, or perverse willful revisionism without which modern poetry as such could not exist.
>
> (Bloom, 1973, p. 30)

When Bloom describes the poet's work as one of "self-saving caricature, of distortion, of perverse willful revisionism," he can also be describing the painter's relationship to the work of his predecessors, the work on which he will be assessed, compared, and judged. If the painter does not meet the quality, excitement, and vigor of his precursors, his work will pass as surely as he will. It will neither compete nor will it make it to the next generation or beyond.

Yet, the anxiety is real. It is what McFarlane (1985) has named the originality paradox, the place where an artist seeks to excel and adhere to the tradition she is entering. The artist who only follows does not meet the level of her own role model. The predecessor, master, achieved that status by making some contribution to the discipline that had not been there before—a contribution that was new, original, even though grounded in or springing from the tradition.

> The relation of the poet to his precursor is conceived by Bloom to be analogous to that of the growing son to his father, that is, an ambivalence of acceptance and rejection. (p. 13)

It would also seem that Bloom, with his emphasis on "distortion" and "perverse willful revisionism," is describing Picasso's revisions of Velázquez's *Las Meninas*, Manet's *Le Déjeuner sur l'herbe*, and Delacroix's *Women of Algiers* (Wollheim, 1987). He makes caricatures of the men and women in Manet's provocative masterpiece. The little princess of King Philip of Spain's family becomes the subject of playful revisions and joyfully tense marks of paint (Gimenez, 2012).

The art historian Jonathan Weinberg (2001) asks what it is that Jackson Pollock attempts to escape by going into the painting, not so much painting upon a surface as much as painting physically in the space. He speculates that what Pollock is attempting to escape is the influence of his artistic fathers, Thomas Hart Benton and Picasso. He discusses this possibility in relation to Bloom's theory of influence and in relation to the notion that one of the functions of modern art is the "projection of the self onto an object" (p. 31). How, he asks, can the modern artist adhere to the tenets of Modernism by projecting only his inner energies and be loyal to his teachers? His conclusion is that the artist's love for his teacher creates a state of ambivalence, an ongoing Oedipal complex or perennial anxiety of influence.

> But the artist cannot generate his art from nothing. He needs influence, even as the child needs his parents. To put it another way, the more an artist finds what he wants to say in another artist's work, the less he is able to say himself. In this way the "love" of the artist for the work of his teacher may be ambivalent, involving both attraction and a longing for escape. (p. 31)

I would take it even further to say that the "love" is not just for the work of the teacher, but for the teacher. This takes the conflict to a Freudian level. How can one love and reject at the same time? How can one meet the desire of the loved one for loyalty and the demands of the society for separation?

Kinds of Copying or Copying

Artists have always and do continue to copy the work of predecessors and peers. Here, I define the kinds of copying I have identified and give reasons for the practice. While it is robust, it is not complete, for I am sure there are reasons I have not identified nor understood.

As a Way of Reaching Larger Audiences

Great paintings were copied in the past as a means of disseminating their image (Tinterow & Lacambre, 2003). The wonders of a painting by Francisco José de Goya y Lucientes could be seen only by the few fortunate enough to be before it. Engraved copies of the painting were made, printed, and distributed for the purpose of having the image—and hence its meaning, subject—reach a larger audience. Before the age of photographs, photographic reproductions in mass-produced books, and electronic imagery, this practice brought the work of master artists all across Europe and beyond.

Many were now able to enjoy some of the qualities of the paintings and sculptures copied. For artists wishing to learn about form, composition, light, and characters in history, it was an invaluable resource. Wilson-Bareau (2003) notes that "Even while Goya was still in Spain, one of his most ardent French admirers had been studying his prints in Paris. Eugene Delacroix was copying figures from the *Caprichos* as early as 1818 or 1819" (p. 151).

For Tradition

The continuation of a tradition of a discipline, craft, practice, or belief results in its continuation and growth, if not in quality, then in forms. Anfam (1990) describes Gorky's decision to apprentice himself to the masters of his craft, painting, both near and far in time as a decision to continue the tradition. It was a conscious choice by Gorky who valued the tradition of painting to submit himself to learning that tradition. His goal as an artist was to continue the tradition of great painters, not break it. Just as McFarland (1985) describes the originality paradox as being present in all great artists, the paradox of coming from a tradition and contributing something new, original, to the same, Gorky resolved. His submission to learning resulted in his being able to contribute to the ongoing dialogue of centuries of painting.

> So thoroughly was Gorky immersed in the narrative which he felt bound to extend-nothing less than that of modern art itself-that over the next ten years or so he eschewed all conventional lipservice to originality. His techniques appeared crafted in the same sense as when an artisan empathizes with a chosen master.... Yet his own voice emerged.
>
> (Anfam, 1990, p. 58)

The emergence of one's own voice after years of disciplined submission to a master and a craft is what Pan (2007) describes in her work studying the traditions of copying in the Eastern and Western traditions. Pan notes that in the Eastern tradition, copying and studying with a master are the truest routes to full participation in the discipline and offer the possibility of an original contribution through a continuance, not break, with tradition. Posterity is accomplished.

The great capoeira master, Mestre João Grande, speaks of preserving the art of capoeira by keeping the traditions of the past masters alive and building upon them with our own creativity. He once told me in 2010 that 50% of the moves he teaches came from his master, Mestre Pastinha. The other 50% he created, in part by studying nature and the movement of animals, the wind's effect on trees, and all forms of nature's displays.

In the film, *Vida Longa*, Mestre Grande plays with Mestre Poncianinho Almedia to demonstrate the continuity of generations in the choreography, music, and improvisation of capoeira, an Afro-Brazilian martial art created by African slaves in Brazil in the 1500s to escape their oppressors. Mestre Poncianinho (2012), who is nearly 50 years younger than Mestre Grande, expresses his own respect for learning from the past when he says, "Capoeira of the past should be capoeira of the present in many ways. Only by going back to the past can we improve a little bit of what we are doing now."

In capoeira, one would not say that they are copying the movements of the past, but that they are playing or learning and playing traditional capoeira. Learning here implies learning the movements of the art by doing them as they were done before. In the making of new paintings, one can learn first how paintings were done before.

For Profit

There are two kinds of copying done primarily for profit. The first is the work of the con man, the fraud, trying to profit from the popularity of an artist's work. This refers to the person who copies solely so that he or she can sell the piece as the work of another. It is deceitful and fraudulent and can be extremely profitable. Paintings that have been presented to collectors as being of the hand of Vermeer or El Greco and have found their way into prestigious collections and museums are many.

The second kind of copying done primarily for profit is related to the work of those who copy for prosperity. It is the copying of great works so that others can see them. Lobstein (2003) states that before the invention of the camera, copying for the draftsmen who were engaged in such a task "appears to have been a fundamental financial resource throughout their lives" (p. 328).

Burton (2009) reminds us of the importance of drawings, engravings, etchings, and even paintings made by artists who attended the wealthiest English and European aristocracy on their grand tour. The work of these artists, copies of masterpieces for remembrance and points of conversation, brought the masters' work to new audiences, including artists who saw and assimilated compositions, motifs, and techniques into their own repertoires.

For Learning

> In copying, one is learning to shape the symbols of pictorial ideas, and copying is as necessary a part of an artistic education as learning to write is of a literary education. It is a way of learning technique, and more-it is a way of reading into other and greater artists' conceptions, and of adding them to our own.
>
> (Duncan, 1902, p. 509)

Duncan lays out the two greatest benefits of copying, particularly for the person beginning to enter into a craft: first, it allows for the "learning of technique" and second, it allows for entering into, "reading into" other and, as Duncan writes, "greater artists' conceptions." By intermingling with greater artists, the aspiring or younger artist can reach a maturity that is not possible on his own; the experience and understanding that come from it enter into the artist's own conceptions, adding and expanding thereon. "It is part of a painter's job to learn his craft. Whether his own works endure may be of little importance, but he should carry on the tradition of good craftsmanship for others" (Sloan, 1939, p. 10).

As in any profession or discipline, learning one's craft necessitates the study of those who have made the craft what it is thus far. Sloan's advocacy for the primacy of the "tradition of craftsmanship" over the reputation of the individual, in fact, frees the individual from the burden of self-importance. Sloan's emphasis on the necessity of submission as an entrance fee to a discipline echoes Hughes' (2006) discussion of MacIntyre's (1984) view of excellence in practice.

Arshile Gorky sought to learn his craft by working in the manner of the artists he considered great (Ashton, 1995; Rosenberg, 1962; Schwabacher, 1957). Delacroix copied the engravings of Goya's work for the same reason.

> Through his close study of Goya's etching in numerous sheets of drawings, Delacroix evolved an expressive language that enabled him to blend gritty realism with sinuous energy and a strong sense of the exotic.
>
> (Wilson-Bareau, 2003, p. 154)

Goya himself learned part of his craft "through studying and copying prints; he once described himself as a pupil of Jose Luzan in Saragossa" (p. 141). Wilson-Bareau tells us that it was Luzan who gave the young Goya the finest prints in his collection in order to train his eye and hand through studying and copying. Goya spent four years with Luzan.

Both French painters Matisse and Marquet copied works in the Louvre under the direction of their master teacher, Moreau (Schneider, 1984), just as Cézanne did before them (Rewald, 1986). Is this not a form of experience that becomes internalized and so able to be drawn upon in the future as Dewey (1936) advocates for an engagement of the world in *Art as Experience*? While it is not the natural world that Dewey advocated most for engagement, as did the New England poets of the time, Thoreau and Emerson, the engagement is real and enters into the lived experience of the artist's being.

Duncum (1984) studied the lives of 35 artists to determine if learning to draw necessarily involves copying. He found that almost all of the artists in his study engaged in copying at some point in their development. He studied the biographies, autobiographies, and early works of artists from 1724 to 1900 including Delacroix, Picasso, and Winslow Homer. He states:

> Gombrich's emphasis that the history of image-making is a history of each generation first acquiring the skills of the previous generation is strongly supported by the cases of cross-generational copying. (p. 100)

I have sought to learn to draw the figure by copying: drawings by Leonardo da Vinci that I saw in San Francisco in 1988, frescos of Giotto in the Arena Chapel in Padua, Picasso's self-portrait in Paris in 1988, Michelangelo's sculpture in Florence in 1996, and Goya's drawings and paintings on ivory at the Frick Collection in New York in 2007. Though my original impetus was to improve my ability to draw the figure, I came to love this practice of standing before a great work and drawing what I see, so increasing and altering my perception of it. I have felt a communion with the artist. Certainly, my skill in drawing the figure has increased, and so has my sense of light, possibility of line, development of composition, understanding of history, understanding of artists, and use of paint or stone.

As a high school art teacher, I frequently asked my students to do the same when I directed them to visit museums and even draw from reproductions in books in the classrooms. Many students took the challenge with great enthusiasm, particularly when they could choose the image from which to copy and learn. I recall one young man who was so excited about the copy of a Michelangelo drawing in the textbook *Discovering Drawing* that he would bring his friends into the class to show them how it was progressing and what he had accomplished.

Old Done Anew

Gorky copied not only the style of Cézanne, but that of contemporaries whose work he saw as the most advanced: Picasso, Miro, and Matta. While he practiced the traditional apprenticeship from a distance, he did so anew.

By learning from modern artists, just as he did from the old masters, he was expanding the limits of the academic approach. Thus, both old masters and modern painters comprised Gorky's pantheon of "academic" inspiration (Lader, 1993, p. 18).

As a Beginning Point

An artist wants to make a body of work, a painting, and as his subject, he chooses to use the masterpiece of another. The copied painting becomes the artist's object of consideration, point of departure. I contend that this is what Picasso did when he made the series of drawings and paintings after both Manet's *Le Déjeuner sur l'herbe* and Velázquez's *Las Meninas* (Glimcher & Glimcher, 1986; Rubin, 1980; Wollheim, 1987). It is also, I suspect, one of the motivations behind Francis Bacon's copies of Van Gogh and Velázquez (Seipel, Steffen, & Vitali, 2004).

Gilmour (1986) points to Picasso's *Les Demoiselles d'Avignon* as an example of an artist modifying an inherited schema, as Gombrich believed all artists do. In this case, Picasso's painting, and the many smaller paintings and drawings that supported it, come from a modification of the visual schema of Cézanne's *Bathers* (Rewald, 1986), the completion of which preceded his own work by only two years.

Robert De Niro Sr. (Swain, 2012) copied Delacroix in postcard form after seeing the paintings in the Louvre. During the time he spent in France to study the great artists of his passion, painting, he painted studies of their works. Well, he did not really copy; he copied with the intent of playing with the forms and images and the French master whose tradition he so admired.

In 2001, some 13 years after I had made drawings of Giotto's frescos, I decided to enlarge my sketches of his frescos, crop the image, and begin a series of paintings. What had begun in 1988 as an effort to study the work of a master in depth and improve my drawing skills became the source for a series of paintings that considered not only the work of Giotto, but my own Catholic background and interest in the sexual content of the work, the relationships between Jesus and Judas and between Jesus and his mother.

As Sloan (1939) states, "The artist has to find something in or about life which interests him" (p. 21). Without doubt, Velázquez's work interested Picasso and Bacon just as Giotto's fresco; their beauty, blue sky, and narrative dramatic human subject interest me. While I suspect that this is not exactly what Sloan meant, there is a life in the work of predecessors and an artist may well find that is the thing "which most interests him."

The artist and founder of The Printmaking Workshop in New York City, Robert Blackburn, is quoted as saying:

We must see this [collaboration] as a hierarchy of relationships in which the mind, thought, expressiveness, imagination, mystery, and magical are dreams of the artist. Without the total awareness of this fact there is no dream space. To become a breathing life force, the artistic ingredient must be felt rather than just used as a display of surfaces, textures, and colors— beautiful but lacking substance. The work must dance on the edge of the abyss.

(Barnet, 1997, back cover)

Having worked on my art and assisted others at Bob's printshop for two years, I feel I have observed and conversed with Bob enough to verify that he lived his life that way, dancing on the edge of the abyss, and it was marvelous!

As a Competition

This sort of attempt to recreate a work famous in antiquity is typical of the period, combining a reverence for ancient models with a challenge to them.

(Museum of Fine Arts, 2009)

So reads the wall placard for a Titian painting, *Venus Rising from the Sea*, in an exhibition at the Museum of Fine Arts in Boston. As long ago as Renaissance Venice and with as prestigious and gifted a painter as Titian, competition was an essential part of the practice and combined with reverence for the accomplishments of those with whom one competes. I would say that the greatest practitioners of any craft are acutely aware of the accomplishments of those who carried the craft before and of the need to compete with such greatness to establish oneself.

It is truly hard to imagine that Picasso and Bacon were not in a duel to the death with their predecessors, especially Picasso with his Spanish competitor, Velázquez. In the end that never comes, who will be crowned the greatest Spanish painter? How frequently did this question plague Picasso? Are not his late paintings, those of the last decade of his life, full of mockery?

They seem to not only mock Velázquez, but they mock the artist himself for caring to duel with a dead man. Smith (2009) writes about the mosqueteiro paintings of Picasso's last years, "Extravagantly clothed and mustachioed, they present an opportunity for excoriating self-portraiture disguised as caricature, while also dueling with past masters like Velázquez, Manet and Rembrandt" (p. E5). Smith also believes that Picasso was competing not only with the masters of the past, those painters he loved, but that he was consciously competing with his contemporaries, although he was in his 90s and living a secluded life in his villa in the south of France.

In discussing Picasso's variations on Velázquez's *Las Meninas,* Galassi (2013) said that "Variation is a time honored tradition that is both homage and parody." She also described Picasso's paintings after Velázquez that he began when he was 75 years old as "a journey." This journey would be one through the painting of Velázquez itself and through Picasso's many feelings toward the master which likely included deep admiration and a desire to vanquish the master through competition in paint played out across centuries.

Galassi noted that Picasso first saw *Las Meninas* when he was 14 and his father took him to see it at The Prado Museum in Madrid as the family was going on vacation. Picasso's father, a drawing teacher who tutored his son beginning at age 3, must have wanted his son to see the greatest works ever and so let these play in his mind. Galassi said that Picasso again saw the painting two years later at the age of 16 when he was a student at The Royal Academy. For more than 60 years, Velázquez played free in Picasso's mind, stirring admiration, humility, ambition, fear, and rivalry.

As a Source of Meditation

> This would be a somewhat superficial mode of understanding the procedure of the artist, who never in reality makes a stroke with his brush without having previously seen it with his imagination; and if he has not yet seen it, he will make the stroke, not in order to externalize his expression (which does not yet exist), but as a kind of experiment and in order to have a point of departure for further meditation and internal concentration.
>
> (Croce, 1966, p. 103)

Here Benedetto Croce notes that the painter may make a stroke upon a support, not to delineate a form or indicate a color or light source, but rather "to have a point of departure." And this point of departure is for what? Why, Croce tells us, it is solely for "further meditation and internal concentration." This leads to what I would ask: Why does it lead to more marks and more meditation and concentration, and then a painting?

Might not Picasso's study of Manet or Degas be like that? Has he, in studying their paintings, found a source upon which to meditate and concentrate? And from such meditation and concentration comes the new work, Picasso's painting. Here, the studying of paintings becomes a meditation upon which the artist builds. Croce continues, stating that this

> point of departure…is like retiring into solitude, or the many other expedients frequently very strange, adopted by artists and scientists, who vary in these according to their various idiosyncrasies. (p. 103)

As an Act of Submission to the Terror of the Sublime

The 18th-century English philosopher Edmund Burke (1958) describes sublimity as resulting from terror or fear in his text, *A Philosophical Enquiry into the Origin of our Ideas of the Sublime and Beautiful.* He states that only before great and potentially dangerous things do we feel the sublime, as it is a result of concern for our well-being before great power.

> [L]et us recollect in what state we have found our minds in escaping some imminent danger, or on being released from the severity of some cruel pain. We have on such occasions found, if I am not much mistaken, the temper of our minds in a tenor very remote from that which attends the presence of positive pleasure; we have found them in a state of much sobriety, impressed with a sense of awe, in a sort of tranquility shadowed with horror. (p. 34)

Did Bacon feel this before Velázquez's painting of Pope Innocent X? When the painter was asked if he went to see Velázquez's *Pope Innocent X* while in Rome, Bacon said he did not. When the interviewer asked "Why?" the painter replied that he had a "fear of seeing the reality of the Velázquez after my tampering with it" (Low, 2005). Now we may guess the nature of his fear, yet fear is how he defined a feeling within himself in relation to a master predecessor. The fear Burke refers to draws our attention because, he argues, it is the most powerful attraction of all. If it was fear of Velázquez's anger at the atrocities done his work, or a fear that Bacon harbored that his own work was so inferior to the model he chose to challenge, or any number of other roots of fear is somewhat irrelevant here, for fear is acknowledged before the master.

Did Picasso feel the sublimity of Poussin's *Rape of the Sabines* (Schiff, 1983) with such passion that he sought to master it through repetition, copy, and dominance? Could we consider the copying of Gorky, Picasso, and Bacon as an effort to enter into the practice, community, and tradition of which MacIntyre (1984) speaks? Do such actions indicate a valuing of virtue that strengthens the tradition of the craft?

The painter, like "The poet confronting his Great Original[,] must find the fault that is not there" (Bloom, 1973, p. 31), and in doing, seeking, so finds something else—something perhaps more true to himself than to the precursor whose work he found it in.

Francis Bacon

"Who, after looking at Bacon for any length of time, can fail to find that the portraits of the king in the Prado look more like Bacon than Bacon?" (Bryson, 1984, p. 46). In the drawing of attention to the past, which is ever present, the artist who copies the work of a predecessor shines a spotlight on it. In the most contemporary analogy, it is like a link on a web page. When one goes to Bacon's imaginary, or not so imaginary, page, there is a link to

Velásquez and the person seeking Bacon, finds his father, Velázquez. Yet as in all father-son relationships, the son is only one half father. "Bacon's relation to Velázquez is intensely cruel: he takes Velázquez own most personal achievement, his bracketing or with-holding of judgment, and annuls it" (p. 46). The son loves the father, adores him, yet must destroy him to live himself, and then so spend his life regretting the action, violence to the one he loves.

Bacon obliterates Pope Innocent X whom Velázquez so disciplined, and sublimely, paints without malice. Velázquez withheld judgment, Bryson believes. Passing not a harsh judgment on the pope with strokes of maliciousness, but rather deferring to posterity, history, and the role of the judge. Velázquez, the master, thinks, yet withholds. Restraint, the sign of greatness is ever present under the tension of the painted surface.

Bacon's restraint, another master, is not in withholding judgment, but in giving reign to his terror. Scarring, slashing, imprisoning Innocent X, yet all within the confines of the canvas, leaving areas sparse, unaffected by the violence, bearing witness to it. The artist's terror of authority, here symbolized by the power of the 16th-century pope, all consuming, universal, is set free, a catharsis, yet controlled as the strokes are upon the pope he has recreated.

> The quality that unites Rembrandt, Velázquez and Bacon across several centuries as great masters of portraiture is their willingness to go to the limits, to walk "along the edge of the precipice" and, if necessary, to break all the rules and to destroy the face in order to get as close as possible to their subject and his or her true appearance.
>
> (Hennig, 2004, p. 219)

Could Bacon and Picasso in their renditions of masters' work anew sought to do the very same as the older masters and "break all the rules and destroy the face" to get ever closer to the point of departure from which the other departed? Certainly, Picasso and Bacon seemed to care little about an insistence upon originality in the art world's superficial understanding of it. In their looking back, though their motivations were certainly different in themselves, could they have sought to find the essence of Velázquez's painting? In so finding the source of the energy, they could bring it into their own canvases, empowering their work and selves.

"For Avery, originality is not a matter of novelty but of rootedness, grasping the source or origin 'of ourselves and things'" (Bjelajac, 1987, p. 4). Is the source, origin, of Bacon, Velázquez? Does Picasso in his last years, seek the "rootedness" of his discipline's father, his compatriot as inventor, master? In seeking "the source," does not the seeker seek strength to create, live in the time they are in with greater resources, the resources of the past?

Interpretations

When Goodman (1976) talks about copying, he states that

> something is wrong with the very notion of copying any of the ways an object is, any aspect of it. For an aspect is not just the object-from-a-given-distance-and-angle-in-a-given-light; it is the object as we look upon or conceive it, a version or construal of the object. (p. 9)

Just as Goodman asserts, the object we see, the one the artist sees when he copies, is "the object as we look upon or conceive it." It is of course something new. It comes from a new source. There is no possibility of a copy, but only a source or a copy in the most open sense. The artist may copy and use the same forms, subjects, compositions, and colors. But in the end, as in the process, the second is as original as the first; only its inspiration was different.

When the master printmaker Judith Solodkin considers an artist's work, be it sculpture, painting, or installations, her goal is to translate the ideas into printmaking. As she said to me in 2006, "You want to translate it, not just copy it." Her goal is to take the artist's essence, content, into the printmaking medium, to help the artist speak in another language, form. When Picasso painted Poussin's or Velázquez's masterpieces again, was he translating the past masters' work into another language, his own? By being of another time, is the language automatically different?

Who Gave the First Model?

> But art can never give the rules that make an art. This is, I believe, the reason why artists in general, and poets principally, have been confined in so narrow a circle; they have been rather imitators of one another than of nature; and this with so faithful an uniformity, and so remote an antiquity, that it is hard to say who gave the first model.
>
> (Burke, 1958, p. 54)

Gombrich (1956) tells us that everything is drawn from a model. There is no invention, but rather a copying of copying of forms and pictorial schema already in the populace, already given form by another long before the one giving form now. When Gombrich was asked, "Well then, where does any new form come from? How is it that the first time something is seen emerged?" he answered, "In the gray areas where coding is optional" (Burton, 2009). That is when new forms are invented, when the old ones no longer serve the needs.

Fiedler

The framework for Fiedler's understanding of artistic activity is provided by his epistemological conviction that reality is not something which we find fully formed in front of us, but is something that we must first bring into existence through our own active contribution. Fiedler rejects mimetically based theories of art, insisting that "Artistic activity is neither slavish imitation, nor arbitrary feeling; rather it is free formative activity". The creation of genuine works of art is based upon a heightened development of perceptual experience, parallel to, but distinct from, the scientific or "conceptual" comprehension of the world. The activity of the artist is none the less genuinely creative in that it brings forth a world which cannot exist apart from this activity.

(Harrison, Wood, & Gaiger, 1998, p. 694)

Harrison et al.'s (1998) discussion of Fiedler's (1876) ideas, as put forth in his essay *On Judging Works of Visual Art*, contains a concept of painting that I argue is why the serious artist's painting based upon the painting of another artist is an engagement with both the medium (the discipline) and the artist, whose piece is the source of the new. For as they state, "The creation of genuine works of art is based upon a heightened development of perceptual experience" (p. 694).

In Picasso's act of making a painting based upon Manet's *Le Déjeuner sur l'herbe*, which is the object of his study, I believe his perception was heightened. One might argue that his engagement with the medium was the same as if he were looking at or thinking of a plate of fruit, remembering a plate of fruit, or trying to simplify what a plate of fruit is and so symbolize it. For the artist copying to learn, pay homage to another, or compete with a master of another time, painting is still painting and demands an engagement with the mind and the medium.

When Fiedler (1876) states that "What art creates is no second world alongside the other world which has an existence without art; what art creates is the world, made by and for the artistic consciousness" (p. 696), he could well be saying that when the artist is apparently copying a work by another artist, he is not. He is creating a "world," a work of his own.

When the painter Milton Resnick said, "My trouble was that I felt I shouldn't be influenced" (Touchman & Dunow, 2006, p. 112), he identified the artist's quandary perfectly: "My trouble." The impulse Resnick speaks of is his attraction to the paintings of both Cézanne and Soutine. Why should they trouble him? Are they not good choices? Of course, that brings up the question: How is a painter to make paintings if he does not look at and admire those made by others? I contend that the whole process, business, of painting is one of imitation, invention, and transformation or even of covering up that imitation inventively. To explain further: a person develops a desire to paint because she has seen paintings, just as a young man may develop a desire to play football because he has seen others playing football.

Now in the process of making and doing, there is, I contend, always a desire to create, invent; that is what makes it fun, desirable to do again. Now the young man sees others playing football and desires to play the same game. He learns to do so by imitating what he sees those in the discipline, sport, doing. Once having mastered, or internalized, the rules and other movements, he invents his own in relation to the rules of the game and the actions of others. It is the same for the painter, singer, and fisherman.

Fiedler's discussion in *On Judging Works of Visual Art* centers not on the copying of works of art, but on the imitation of nature, and if that is even possible, which he contends, rightly so, is not. Yet, I will take his thoughts to the concerns of this book and say that it is no more possible to make an imitation of an already existent painting than it is to make an imitation of a tree already grown. In the act of copying, one is creating, and creating always implies anew by definition.

When Fiedler asked, "But what agreement could exist between the copy and the object itself?" (p. 695), he asked that we consider the magnitude of both the creative process and the distance that lies between two things that is not just one of form correspondence but of purpose and meaning. Both Gombrich (1956) and Malraux (1953) argue that art begins with art, schema, and convention. The work of predecessors directs the work of the contemporary artists. It provides a starting point. Gombrich proposes the notion of making and matching by which he implies that artists do not so much create new forms as they match existing ones, and over time they may change them. One could think of it as a Darwinian process of evolution applied to drawing.

Gombrich (1956) insists that the artist needs a formula, schema, from which to begin. The artist then modifies the schema learned through imitation to suit his expressive intentions. Without such a schema, an artist would not know where to begin. While Gombrich is not focusing specifically on copying for learning, his theory supports the practice, as an artist seeks to learn by first imitating.

Pan (2007) notes the long tradition of artists in the East studying closely with a master and learning through imitation and repetition. The education, training, of the artist is one by which the student learns the methods of his master, and then develops his own style or way of making, based upon his master's training and his own inclinations, gifts. Much like Gombirch's schema of learning, Pan's investigation supports the history of invention coming after imitation.

Arshile Gorky spent easily a decade imitating the artists whom he most admired: Cézanne, Picasso, Kandinsky, and Miro (Ashton, 1995; Rosenberg, 1962; Schwabacher, 1957). He spoke often of the Italian Renaissance painter Paolo Ucello and was known among his circle for having a keen eye for quality and taking friends and students alike around the museums, pointing out what he saw as the greatest qualities in paintings (Schwabacher, 1957).

After this time of chosen apprenticeship, Gorky soared (Ashton, 1995). His paintings broke new ground with the skill of the masters he so admired and now mastered in his own hands. The repertoire of painterly skills and understanding he held in his grasp was immense. His paintings are unlike any seen, yet with the grace, light, energy, and thought of masterpieces from the Renaissance to Modernism. His friend and fellow painter, Stuart Davis, argued that Gorky was always a master and that even in his copies, his paintings were stronger and more original than those of his contemporaries who were contemptuous of his apprenticeship (Rosenberg, 1962).

Hughes (2006) in discussing the work of Alasdair MacIntyre notes "that *subordination* is a necessary step in the process of entering into a practice" (p. 139). He notes that "This perspective shows up in situations where one artist trusts the judgment of another artist. Such convictions have been historically understood as a constitutive aspect of education, apprenticeship, subordination" (p. 137). Gorky chose to subordinate any desire for domination through invention to enter into the practice of painting. The results speak volumes for such a path.

Gorky trusted not just the masters of the distant past, but the artists he considered the most gifted of his day: Picasso, Miro, Kandinsky, Masson, and Matta (Lader, 1993). He copied for the sake of internalizing the qualities he saw in each artist's work that he admired, wanted for his own possession, to be used in his own work, eventually if not immediately. He "could not only imitate Cézanne's style but explain his theories" (p. 18). For Gorky, the act of apprenticeship was total, by which I mean that unlike Bacon whose paintings are in some respects comments upon Velázquez's paintings, Gorky's copying was to become a better painter.

In the Making of a Painting

I contend that in the making of a painting, painting occurs. A painter cannot but engage in painting but as a painter. By this, I mean that though an artist may be copying the forms and composition of another artist, questions arise in the act of painting that must be answered. A mark here; ask which mark goes next to it. Perhaps the answer is none. This color upon this color changed the one adjacent and below. Do I leave it or change it again? The true painter must submit to the demands of the painting, just as the true teacher must submit to the demands and needs of the students.

Merleau-Ponty (1961, in Harrison & Wood, 1993) more eloquently notes the same in his discussion of Panofsky.

> Panofsky shows that the 'problems' of painting which magnetize its history are often solved obliquely, not in the course of inquiries instigated to solve them but, on the contrary, at some point when the painters, having reached an impasse, apparently forget those problems and permit themselves to be attracted by other things. (p. 754)

What "other things" might have Picasso been considering as he painted after Velázquez? Was he thinking about paint itself? Sex, or sexual desire, which is perhaps the main subject of Manet's *Le Déjeuner sur l'herbe*? When did he move from copying compositional elements to creating a somewhat different, more Picasso-like painting?

Baxandall

> I emphasized that the painter's complex problem of good picture-making becomes a serial and continually self-redefining operation, permanent problem-reformulation, as soon as he enters the process of actually painting.
>
> (Baxandall, 1985, p. 73)

When Baxandall writes that the painter's problem, brief as he describes it earlier in his text *Patterns of Intention*, is one of permanent problem-reformulation, he argues for the seeing of Picasso's many paintings based upon Velázquez's *Las Minias* as Picasso's own. Baxandall contends that "as soon as he enters the process of actually painting," the painting process takes over. It is a "self-redefining operation." That operation, process, is one of constantly seeing each action in relation to each previous one and anticipating those actions that are forthcoming. As Picasso painted, his thoughts were primarily with the painting at hand, not the one by Velázquez. To build on this thought, I refer to Clifton Olds (1990), who in his critique of Wollheim's *Painting as an Art*, speaks eloquently of the power of the each mark to change subsequent and future marks and so the whole of a painting, or of a drawing or sculpture.

> I would maintain that, unless a painting is so mathematically conceived as to be totally formulaic, the very process of creation necessarily alters to one degree or another the original conception. This alteration occurs with the placing of each mark upon the surface, and the process is progressive and catalytic-catalytic in the sense that each mark not only enjoys a life of its own but also has an effect upon the artist as well as the ongoing production of the painting. (p. 26)

"The history of art teems with artists who can be fully themselves only after they have made some form of initial submission" (Wollheim, 1987, p. 252). Though Wollheim was speaking about Ingres' need to submit to the changing demands of patrons as the ruling of France went from the monarchy to the Revolution to the Restoration, his point has much broader application, as I am certain he meant it to have. To become oneself, in this case, an artist, requires letting go of the notion of oneself, of self-importance, and submitting to another, be it person or form. In so doing, in the forgetting of one's believed importance, one becomes who one truly is, without consciously trying.

Picasso's extensive study, replications, of Manet's *Le Déjeuner sur l'herbe* number in the hundreds of drawings, more than 25 paintings, and a small group of linoleum cuts (Wollheim, 1987). Picasso's copying of the French master's painting underwent major transformations as one would expect both with Picasso the great inventor and with the numbers involved. The four figures in Manet's painting eventually became three in Picasso's as he omitted one of the men in the original *Déjeuner*. As with most of his paintings, the man can be seen as an image of the self, and so what need did Picasso have for the other man who would be a competitor for the two nude women?

Manet's composition eventually turned vertical, consistent with a portrait and appropriately so as Picasso eliminated most of the landscape that Manet had painted. The transformation of the painting is wonderfully amusing and demanding of our attention. Each painting confirms Picasso's seemingly endless creativity. Wollheim sees these transformations as part of Picasso's process of submitting to Manet, internalizing his painting, and eventually surpassing him, if nowhere else, than in boldness and sheer numbers.

> I began my discussion of the *Dejeuner* series by saying that its fundamental meaning for Picasso was to establish, and then to assert, an identification with one of the past masters of his art, and that this is effected through, rather than despite, the radical transformations that Picasso applied to Manet's composition.
>
> (Wollheim, 1987, p. 246)

When Francis Bacon painted Pope Innocent the X after Velázquez's portraits of the same, what was he doing? Why? And like Picasso, who made so many paintings after Velázquez's *Las Minas*, is it the pull, strength, of the painting that commands the attention of these artists? Does a desire to compete with the master make the artist attempting it even greater?

Could it be that the power of the aesthetic object is so strong that the artist copying seeks the pleasure of entering more fully than looking alone allows? In the process of copying a painting, does the desire to enter into the other artist, master, meet the desire to excel? Subordination gives way to dominance if the new work is successful.

Beardsley (1958) discusses the aesthetic experience as "one in which attention is firmly fixed upon heterogeneous but interrelated components of a phenomenally objective field" (p. 527). Is Picasso's engagement with Velázquez's work first an aesthetic experience? Is he taking in Velázquez's work with the pleasure of a viewer? Does that mindset or engagement change when he goes from observation to creation, mark making, color matching, form creation, and image realization?

Francis Bacon, Again

"Yes, even if they're only copies, a painter should paint" (Archimbaud, 1993, p. 172). Such was the painter Francis Bacon's response to a question about whether he paints every day. While it sounds as if he considered copying a secondary activity, for him, it was frequently primary. Let us take his quote, directive, and consider it. First, he states that a painter should always paint, even if he has no idea of what subject to paint. Second, one can infer that Bacon believed copying to be a valuable activity for a painter to engage in, even if not as valued as another.

Bacon takes Velázquez's painting *Pope Innocent X* and paints it over and over again (Seipel et al., 2004). It looks like the pope is in a birdcage being sucked down into a vacuum in his *Portrait of Pope Innocent X* from 1953. How many times can one man paint the same thing repeatedly when it was not even his idea? Or was it? Maybe Bacon's idea was to paint, make a painting that began with Velázquez's idea, object, painting. That is the subject. The subject is Velázquez.

Is there a difference between when a painter sets up a still life and paints it over and over, or goes in front of Mt. St. Victorie as Cézanne did and paints it time and time again until death claims the artist, or what Bacon did in using Velázquez's painting in the same manner? I would argue yes, but more importantly, no.

In all the above cases, the artist is looking at something and making an impression of it, and so the act is the same. On the other hand, looking at man-made objects and small dead life as Chardin did in painting still life, and looking at mountains rising from the earth as Cézanne did, is different in their scale, place, light, and human formation. How is painting from a painting different? First, it is a painting from the same medium. What I mean is that in painting a still life, the artist is transposing objects made and small natural forms to an image composed of spots of color. In a painting from a painting, the artist is transposing small marks of color to small marks of color. Or is he? Or is he only?

I contend he is dealing with small marks of color, ideas of human destiny, lineage, competition, submission, and assertion. The act of painting, whether while trying to represent the colors and lights that one perceives before her, or in trying to represent another's painting, is much the same—one of applying paint to a surface, color next to color. Destiny is what an artist thinks about in part as a reason for making. Is it her destiny to be a great painter, to be in a lineage of painters? Competition is large and takes in competing with oneself, one's past work, competing not to compete, competing certainly with one's peers and in the timelessness of art considered in an intellectual space where there are no constraints of time, and in death one competes equally with predecessors.

Submission is crucial. Eventually, one lets go. The painter submits to the success or failure of the painting, to her perception of her standing in the field, or most graciously perceived to be the eloquence of another. Before, after, and before submission comes assertion. The asserting personality comes back and speaks again: "I am here!" "I challenge you!"

Martin Kippenberger challenged his self-image while he paid reverence and mockery to other artists in a series of large, painted self-portraits in the guise of his famous predecessors. One painting that was on view at the Museum of Modern Art depicts the artist in a stance taken from a photograph of Picasso in his boxer-short underwear only.

Francis Bacon's place as one of the greatest painters, or at least image makers—for I contend that is his greatest gift—of the 20th century is as secure as is his relationship to the painting masters of the past. He created painting upon painting of Pope Innocent the X based upon Velázquez's portrait from the 1500s. They make us aware of Velázquez's painting and of the distance, dissonance, between them, between both the paintings and the painters themselves.

Kimmelman (2008), in discussing a retrospective of Francis Bacon's paintings, notes the artist's increasing appeal in the last decade to wider audiences and especially younger artists and historians. He writes:

> his work translates quite easily to a new century. So does the sweaty sex and violence, luxuriant but couched in aloofness and guided, always, by grand allusions to old masters and learned texts. (p. E5)

Those "old masters" can be easily identified in Bacon's oeuvre as his reimaging and repainting of their work to a new century are evident. What is most interesting or ironic in relation to the notions of originality and newness is that Bacon did not care. That is the popular image of the man. He did not care what people thought. His studio was a hovel, he drank daily, and his gallery gave him money in cash intermittently as if he were receiving an allowance. He copied Velázquez because something in the Spanish master's work drew him to it. Bacon's achievement in his painting and then in the art world came not through studying in a school of any kind, but through painting and studying the masters (Seipel et al., 2004).

Even when discussing his painting of the triptych *Three Studies for Figures at the Base of a Crucifixion*, Bacon would contend, "Well of course, you're working then on your own feelings and sensations, really" (Gamper, 2004, p. 329). Bacon emphasized that even when working on a crucifixion which has been painted thousands of times throughout European history and using the format of the altarpiece, a triptych, the painter's thoughts and feelings were his "own."

Through the study of Bacon's crucifixion and triptychs, which came from his study of earlier ones, I realized that I painted my own apparently much more abstract triptych that I titled *Crucifixion*. Upon waking from a nap in my studio, I saw in the arrangement of the paintings on the wall both a triptych and a crucifixion. Would I have seen this had I not been studying Bacon as well as discussing Renaissance altarpieces with my students?

Gamper (2004) believes that Bacon's variations of Van Gogh's paintings, such as the Dutch artist's *The Painter on the Road to Tarascon*, are an effort to enter into Van Gogh's "approach to reality" (p. 295). Bacon was not seeking a lesson in formal composition or color approaches but sought to enter into an admired artist's psyche at work, to imitate his experience of reality, not the product of that experience.

> Here Bacon is trying to express what art is all about for him. He has to try to make truth accessible through his art, but he cannot do this by simply imitatively reproducing what he sees. The highest goal is the revelation of a truth that surpasses reality in its truthfulness. (p. 295)

Van Gogh's landscapes were like bodies to Bacon (van Alphen, 2004). Bacon painted his figures in the center of his massive canvases, wrestling and making love, with the physicality that Van Gogh used to paint the fields of southern France, the sunflowers, and even the postman. Such are the qualities that one artist can see, absorb, and study in another's work.

The French School

> Odilon Redon once borrowed a Cézanne painting of a bouquet from his patron and friend Andre Bonger. He kept it for four days and copied it.... Redon admired Cézanne's talent.
>
> (Schneider, 1984, p. 108)

The admiration one artist has for another's talent may compel him to seek to master that talent through copying, because copying takes looking to another level. Every painter looks at paintings and if it is one a painter admires, he thinks about how the paint was applied. The painter can feel the movement of the brush in the body. He can look at the layers of paint and consider the transparency, and internalize the composition. Yet by copying the painting, the painter studies it unconsciously, for while he is doing this, body and mind internalize what is being done.

Courbet sets up a paradox, a contradiction. He stated in a letter of 1861 that art is individual and cannot be taught (Harrison et al., 1998), and he nurtured a public image of intense individualism and rebellion against the reigning school of art, yet he himself studied with men who were considered masters in his hometown of Ornans, France, and in both Paris and Besancon. Yet, Chilvers (2003) believes that Courbet "learnt more from copying the work of 17th-century naturalist such as Caravaggio and Velázquez in the Louvre" (p. 145). In the same letter where he stated he "could not think of setting myself up as a teacher to be imitated" (Harrison et al., 1998, p. 403), he goes on to state that he would be glad to assist in the "setting up of a common studio, which would hark back to the most fertile collaborations of the Renaissance"

(p. 404). The artists of the Renaissance apprenticed for many years with a master (Hart, 1987).

The Louvre has served as the great school of French painters. Cézanne, like Courbet before him, made copies of works there (Rewald, 1986). Both these painters were considered strongly independent of the schools of painting most popular during their time, and both chose to apprentice themselves to the ones they considered masters. Great artists need not look to peers but to those who have achieved the most, and those who are frequently in the past, not contemporaneous with them.

Matisse's Long Apprenticeship

"I have never avoided the influence of others. I would have considered this a cowardice and a lack of sincerity toward myself," Matisse told the poet and art critic Apollinaire when the artist was in his early 40s (Schneider, 1984, p. 720). I find it hard to see such influence in Matisse's work. To me, it is all Matisse. The paintings are such. The cut-outs of his later years are most certainly the artist's invention.

Schneider (1984) in his extensive work *Matisse* notes that the length of time—five years—Matisse spent in the studio of his master, Moreau, was just a small part of a 15-year apprenticeship during which the artist tried to learn all of the history of painting up to his own time. The author concludes that Matisse's "rigorous, 15-year-long apprenticeship was an essential background to the desire and ability to forget everything in the explosion of Fauvism" (p. 720).

As Bloom (1973) writes, "No poet since Adam and Satan speaks a language free of the one wrought by his precursors" (p. 25). Matisse's effort to learn the language of his discipline, tradition, bore great fruit. Schneider tells us that for a four-year period, Matisse was absorbed in the study of Cézanne. Thus it is that an artist searches for himself in the work of his great predecessors.

Giotto and I—How I Came to Paint Angels, Saints, and Christ

As I wrote earlier, I sought to improve my drawing, and particularly of the human figure, by standing in front of frescos, drawings, paintings, and sculptures, and copying them. In 1988, I filled many pages of a sketchbook I had with drawings of Giotto's frescos at the Arena Chapel in Padua, Italy. During the days I was there, I got up early in the morning to draw when my mind was most alert and to have the chapel largely to myself to consider Giotto.

I did come to draw better. Many years later, when seeking a subject for painting, I turned to the sketchbook, and from the sketches of Jesus and Mary, Judas and angels I had made from Giotto's frescos, I made anew large paintings of *The Lamentation* and *The Kiss*. Angels fly in small canvases. From here, I continued my interest in religious subjects and painted Saint Sebastian hung with arrows on a tree, and made a series of monotypes from my own lithograph of St. Michael slaying the devil.

The journey I have spoken of above, where artists copy for so many reasons, I have walked and still do. Eagerly, I await the next master drawing show to stand before and draw. I hope that a trip to Italy will happen soon so that I can draw Masaccio's *The Expulsion of Adam and Eve* in the Brancacci Chapel in Florence. And in truth, before the religious paintings, I was copying the motion and movement of the abstract expressionists Jackson Pollock and Willem de Kooning and studying the exquisite intellect and forms of Arshile Gorky.

Student and Father

"Cut it. Glue it. Learn it." That is what Hisao Hanafusa (2007) said to me when I asked him if he was showing his 14-year-old son Sen how to make furniture without nails or glue in the ancient Japanese manner that Mr. Hanafusa does and learned from his father, who learned it from his, and who learned it from his. Mr. Hanafusa, who is in his 70s or 80s, is a painter and furniture maker who came from Japan to New York City some 45 years ago. Mr. Hanafusa's furniture sells for tens of thousands of dollars to people like the actor Harrison Ford, whom he had never heard of.

Mr. Hanafusa also told me that he sends his son to Japan during the summer to be with monks, who rise at 5:00 in the morning. His son cleans the floor and watches. This is his father's expectation. Learning can take place without a word.

Artists

George Nick (2006) gives credit for his success as a painter to his teacher, Edwin Dickinson. He began his lecture at the Vermont Studio Center in the summer of 2006 by saying that Dickinson was his teacher at the Art Students League for five years. Although he then went to Yale University, he credits his ability to paint anything to his mentor: "Dickinson gave me the tools to paint anything."

That was 50 years before I met him. In his studio in Massachusetts hangs a painting from a half-century ago about which he said, "That's when I was painting like Dickinson." Also in his studio, alongside the paintings he did only days before, is a portrait he painted of his father. There are also photos of his wife and daughter, his life now, and the portrait of his father, his life from where he began. His life as a painter began with a master, Dickinson.

"If you really want to feel bad, copy a master. That's when you know what a master is," Nick told the audience in Vermont. And Picasso copied the paintings of Velázquez and Poussin when he was in his 80s (Schiff, 1983). And

Cézanne always drew from the sculptures in the Louvre when he was in Paris (Rewald, 1986).

Capoeiristas

When one entered the Capoeira Angola Center on West 14th Street in New York City, one first saw a large, 18 × 24 photograph of Mestre Pastinha above an altar with candles, flowers, and so many other items of meaning. This was the academy of Mestre João Grande, who has received innumerable awards and honors including the National Heritage Fellowship from the National Endowment for the Arts, and whom the Smithsonian Institution has recorded. He has been an honored guest and participant at capoeira centers in New Zealand, Mexico, Germany, and cities across the United States. He has given workshops in Japan, Croatia, Los Angeles, Brazil, and Italy.

He reveres his teacher and tells his students to honor the great tradition of capoeira Angola as taught to him by Mestre Pasthina and that he entrusts them to continue. He does not refer students to himself, although that is why we are all there, from South America, Europe, Asia, and New York City. He maintains the altar to his mestre with great love. He burns incense, lights candles, and replaces flowers in the mornings with his prayers.

The reverence goes to those who have taught us and to the discipline being taught, of which each practitioner is only one link—hopefully a strong link—to the centuries before and to those hopefully to follow. Mestre Morae is considered one of the greatest students of Mestre Grande. One verse in his song titled Tradicao goes: "whoever doesn't have a father or a master/also doesn't have any tradition." Marks (2001) in his notes to the song states that "the master's name functions like a passport in the world of capoeira, and without it, the capoeirista would be a nobody" (p. 26). In capoeira, as I contend in painting, everyone wants to know who was someone's master. Without a master, a person is no one, a fake.

During a class at Mestre Grande's academy, Mario Pereira (2008), who was teaching in our mestre's absence, instructed the students to melt into our opponent partner's movements and so neutralize him. Is copying a work of art a way to neutralize it, absorb its energy?

A Painter Next Door, Both Our Teachers

Some years ago, when I was seeking a studio to rent, I entered the studio of a painter whom I did not know, as he thought he might be leaving his own space. We spoke of rent and time, not artist or teachers. Yet, when I was in his studio, I felt a familiar energy. His name is Henry Finkelstein. Some weeks later, I read his biography on a website and realized that the painting professor that he names as having studied with was also mine, although seven or so years later. Our mutual painting teacher, master, was Nicholas Marsciano and we both also studied with Rueben Kadish at The Cooper Union.

I have entered many artists' studios, but never did I recognize an energy as familiar as I did in his. I contend that somehow the energy from Marsciano went to Henry and I could feel it when I was in Henry's studio, even though I never knew him or anything about him before I entered.

During my senior year studying painting at The Cooper Union, I worked with Nic Marsciano. We spoke easily and enjoyed each other's company. He always challenged me and was not always gentle. He had more insight into painting than any painting instructor I had spoken to before. Can the energy of a teacher go from student to student and exist in each, or all?

In Ending, Continuing

From what I have seen children do, copy, and learn; from my reading and scholarly research; and from my observations of human behavior—what people do, I say with confidence that copying is one of the truest and most logical ways of learning. I also say with the knowledge I have drawn from the same sources that originality cannot be held back. The new will be. The drive to create, which I believe is the initial impetus to copy, continues beyond the act of copying. Edmund Burke nearly 300 years ago in 1757 wrote about the dual impulses within us to both imitate and excel more elegantly than I:

> Although imitation is one of the great instruments used by providence in bringing our nature towards its perfection, yet if men gave themselves up to imitation entirely, and each followed the other, and soon in an eternal circle it is easy to see that there could never be any improvement amongst them.... To prevent this, God has planted in man a sense of ambition from the contemplation of his excelling his fellows of something deemed valuable amongst them. (p. 50)

References

Anfam, D. (1990). *Abstract expressionism*. London, UK: Thames and Hudson.

Archimbaud, M. (1993). *Francis Bacon: In conversation*. London, UK: Phaidon.

Ashton, D. (1980). *A fable of modern art*. New York, NY: Thames and Hudson.

Ashton, D. (1995). A straggler's view of Gorky. In M. Auping (Ed.), *Arshile Gorky: The breakthrough years* (pp. 39–61). New York, NY: Rizzoli International.

Ayrton, M. (1960). In K. E. Maison (Ed.), *Art themes and variations: Five centuries of interpretations and re-creations*. New York, NY: Harry N. Abrams.

Bal, M. (1999). *Quoting Caravaggio: Contemporary art, preposterous history*. Chicago, IL: University of Chicago Press.

Barnet, W. (1997). *Will Barnet, Bob Blackburn: An artistic friendship in relief*. LaGrange, GA: Cochran Collection.

Baxandall, M. (1985). *Patterns of intention: On the historical explanation of pictures.* New London, CT: Yale University Press.

Beardsley, M. (1958). *Aesthetic: Problems in the philosophy of criticism.* New York, NY: Harcourt, Brace.

Bjelajac, D. (1987). *Eric Avery: Healing before art.* Texas: Corpus Christi State University.

Bloom, H. (1973). *The anxiety of influence; A theory of poetry.* New York, NY: Oxford University Press.

Bryson, N. (1984). *Tradition and desire: From David to Delacroix.* Cambridge, UK: Cambridge University Press.

Burke, E. (1958). *A philosophical enquiry into the origin of our ideas of the sublime and beautiful.* New York, NY: Columbia University Press. (First published 1757).

Burton, J. (2009) Discussions with the author. New York, NY.

Chilvers, I. (2003). *The concise Oxford dictionary of art and artists* (3rd ed.). Oxford, UK: Oxford University Press.

Croce, B. (1966). *Aesthetic: As science of expression and general linguistics.* New York, NY: Noon Day Press.

Dewey, J. (1936). *Art as experience.* New York, NY: Perigee.

Duncan, J. (1902). Art. *The Elementary School Teacher and Course of Study, 2*(7), 508–512.

Duncum, P. (1984). How 35 children born between 1724 and 1900 learned to draw. *Studies in Art Education, 26*(2), 92–102.

Fiedler, C. (1949). *On judging works of visual arts.* (H. S. Simmern and F. Mood, trans.). Berkely. CA: University of California Press. (Original work published 1876).

Galassi, S. (2013). *Lecture: Picasso's variations on the masters in black and white.* New York, NY: Guggenheim Museum.

Gamper, V. (2004). Bacon's realism after Van Gogh. In W. Seipel, B. Steffen, & C. Vitali (Eds.), *Francis Bacon and the tradition of art.* Basel, Switzerland: Skira.

Gilmour, J. (1986). *Picturing the world.* Albany, NY: State University of New York Press.

Gimenez, C. (Ed.) (2012). *Picasso black and white.* New York, NY: The Guggenheim Museum.

Glimcher, A. B., & Glimcher, M. (Eds.). (1986). *Je suis le cahier: The sketchbooks of pablo picasso.* Boston, MA: Atlantic Monthly Press.

Gombrich, E. H. (1956). *Art and illusion: A study in the psychology of pictorial representation.* Princeton, NJ: Princeton University Press.

Goodman, N. (1976). *Languages of art: An approach to a theory of symbols.* Indianapolis, IN: Bobbs-Merrill.

Hanafusa, H. (2007, March 23). Discussion with the author. Long Island City, NY.

Harrison, C., & Wood, P. (1993). *Art in theory 1900-1990: An anthology of changing ideas.* London, UK: Blackwell.

Harrison, C., Wood, P., & Gaiger, J. (1998). *Art in theory 1815-1900: An anthology of changing ideas.* London, UK: Blackwell.

Hart, F. (1987). *History of Italian renaissance art: Painting, sculpture, architecture* (3rd ed.). New York, NY: Abrams.

Hennig, A. (2004). Francis Bacon: Portraiture after representation. In W. Seipel, B. Steffen, & C. Vitali (Eds.), *Francis Bacon and the tradition of art.* Basel, Switzerland: Skira.

Hughes, B. S. (2006). *The moral nature of artistic genius.* Unpublished dissertation, EdD, Teachers College, Columbia University, New York, NY.

Kennel, S. (2003). Bearden's musee imaginaire. In R. Fine (Ed.), *The art of Romare Bearden*. Washington, DC: The National Gallery of Art.

Kimmelman, M. (2008). Chivalrous bad boy's messy world. *The New York Times*, September 25, p. E5.

Lader, M. (1993). *Arshile Gorky*. New York, NY: Abbeville.

Lobstein, D. (2003). Appendix I: Nineteenth-century French copies after old masters. In B. Tinterow & G. Lacambre (Eds.), *Manet/Velázquez: The French taste for Spanish painting*. New York, NY: The Metropolitan Museum.

Low, A. (2005). [Director] *Bacon's arena: An art of pain and beauty*. British Broadcasting Corporation, England.

MacIntyre, A. C. (1984). *After virtue: A study in moral theory* (2nd ed.). Indianapolis, IN: University of Indiana Press.

Malraux, A. (1953). *The voices of silence*. (S. Gilbert, trans.). New York, NY: Doubleday.

Marks, M. (2001). *Notes to the recording Capoeira Angola 2: Brincando na roda*. Washington, DC: Smithsonian Folkways Recordings.

McFarland, T. (1985). *Originality and imagination*. Baltimore, MD: The John Hopkins University Press.

Museum of Fine Arts Boston. (2009). Wall placard in the exhibition, "Titian, Tintoretto, Veronese: Rivals in Renaissance Venice". Boston, MA: Author.

Nick, G. (2006). Lecture at the Vermont Studio Center. Johnson, VT.

Olds, C. (1990). Wollheim's theory of artist as spectator: A complication. *Journal of Aesthetic Education, 24*(2), 25–30.

Pan, Q. (2007). *Creativity within copying: A comparative study of copying as a way of learning in Euro-American painting and Chinese painting traditions*. Unpublished dissertation. EdD, Teachers College, Columbia University, New York, NY.

Pereira, M. (2008). *Class lecture*. New York, NY: Capoiera Angola Center of Mestre João Grande.

Poncianinho, M. (2012). *Vida Longa*. London, England: Bertie Films.

Rewald, J. (1986). *Cézanne*. New York, NY: Harry N. Abrams.

Rosenberg, H. (1962). *Arshile Gorky: The man, the time, the idea*. New York, NY: The Sheep Meadow Press/Flying Point Books.

Rubin, W. (1980). *Pablo Picasso, a retrospective*. New York, NY: The Museum of Modern Art.

Sartre, J. P. (1962). An explication of *the stranger*. In G. Bree (Ed.), *Camus: A collection of critical essays*. Englewood Cliffs, NJ: Prentice-Hall.

Schiff, G. (1983). *Picasso: The last years, 1963-1973*. New York, NY: George Braziller.

Schneider, P. (1984). *Matisse*. (M. Taylor and B. Stevens Romer, trans.). New York, NY: Rizzoli.

Schwabacher, E. K. (1957). *Arshile Gorky*. New York, NY: Macmillan.

Seipel, W., Steffen, B., & Vitali, C. (Eds.). (2004). *Francis Bacon and the tradition of art*. Basel, Switzerland: Skira.

Simmons, S. (2008). Cultivating creativity in arts education: Myths, misconceptions, and practical procedures. In *Teaching standards-based creativity in the arts*. The South Carolina Alliance for Arts Education.

Sloan, J. (1939). *Gist of art*. New York, NY: Dover.

Smith, R. (2009). Going all out, right to the end. *The New York Times*, April 17, p. E5.

Swain, M. (2012). Robert De Niro in context. Lecture at the New York Studio School, March 28.

Tinterow, B., & Lacambre, G. (2003). *Manet/Velázquez: The French taste for Spanish painting*. New York, NY: The Metropolitan Museum of Art.

Touchman, M., & Dunow, E. (2006). *Soutine and modern art*. New York, NY: Cheim & Read.

van Alphen, E. (2004). Reconcentration: Bacon reinventing his models. In W. Seipel, B. Steffen, & C. Vitali (Eds.), *Francis Bacon and the tradition of art*. Basel, Switzerland: Skira.

Weinberg, J. (2001). *Ambition and love in modern American art*. New Haven, CT: Yale University Press.

Wilson-Bareau, J. (2003). Manet and Spain. In B. Tinterow & G. Lacambre (Eds.), *Manet/Velázquez: The French taste for Spanish painting*. New York, NY: The Metropolitan Museum of Art.

Wittgenstein, L. (1972). *On certainty*. (G. E. M. Ansome & G. H. von Wright, Eds.; D. Paul & G. E. M. Ansome, trans.). New York, NY: Harper Torchbooks.

Wollheim, R. (1987). *Painting as an art*. Princeton, NJ: Princeton University Press.

4   The Method of the Interviews

In this chapter, I discuss the method of the interviews and the rationale behind interview research and autoethnography as these were two of the methods which form the basis of this book.

> Through the *Thou* a man becomes *I*. That which confronts him comes and disappears, relational events condense, then are scattered, and in the change consciousness of the unchanging partner, of the *I*, grow clear and each time stronger.
>
> (Buber, 1958, p. 28)

It is through speaking, interviewing, asking questions, and listening for responses that I hoped to learn some more about the relationship of artists to their mentors, and if copying in the largest sense played a role in that relationship or in their development at all. This was an interview study, which is where the researcher interviews individuals who have knowledge and experiences that can shed light on or bring about insights into a question, problem, or phenomenon.

This study was also an autoethnography as I looked backward and forward to my own development as an artist, and it is from my living as an artist that I came to this work. It is the specificity of a thing that makes it special, which makes it the thing itself. Here, the specificity of the thing, the method, was that the researcher was an artist speaking with other artists. In researching the ways of the developing of the artists in this study and in history as determined through a wide look at the history of the art, I read biographies and studies and thought backwards on my own history of development and of those who influenced and helped me. With all this said, the method was in part a way of researching the self through others and others through the self.

By this, I mean that while I spoke with four artists and listened and considered their words, I compared and considered what they said also in relation to my own experience of developing into the artist I sought to be and am now called by others. The term autoethnography would best describe one way in

DOI: 10.4324/9781003451303-4

which I have worked here, one method in this qualitative study on the ways and habits of artists, of which I am one.

Method of Inquiry

Four artists were interviewed following an interview guide that was designed to elicit their thoughts on their development as artists and to what extent mentors played a role in that development: if copying either the works or ways of others contributed to that development, if the artist looked to a person from history for guidance, that is, had a mentor in the mind, and if the artists interviewed had been a mentor to others. The interviews were transcribed and noted for similarities and differences. Some additional questions were later posed to the artists whose answers helped to clarify responses during the first interview.

The questions of the interview guide were designed to draw responses from the participants that would help to answer the research questions. They were also designed and sequenced in a manner that allowed me and the participants to gradually enter into the discussion and concepts seeking responses. Such a way of structuring an interview was demonstrated by Dr. Anna Neumann (2010) in her class on interview research as well as discussed in the writings of Kvale (1996) and Maxwell (1992).

What the artists said was also considered in relation to the history of the mentor and disciple relationship in the development of artists, as ascertained through historical readings discussed in the literature review of the previous chapter. What one artist noted and another did not, and where three of the four artists cited a similar influential experience were discussed. Similarities and differences were considered. The place of copying in the work of artists and in their manners, by which I mean intention to try to be similar to another, was also considered historically and within this group of four artists who are part of history themselves.

Historical information on how artists have developed derived from the literature review was considered in forming the interview guide. The research questions, the reason for the study, provided the framework and goal for the interview questions. Each person speaks in her own way. As each artist spoke differently—that is, some answered questions most directly, while others spoke in larger personal narratives—the follow-up questions posed to each artist differed, though not in substance.

The four artists I interviewed were chosen because they had demonstrated throughout their adult lives a commitment to making and exhibiting art, to being artists. Three of the four were known to me as colleagues and fellow artists whose work I respect. Two had spoken of mentors in their lives in our previous discussions before any thought of this book came to be. The artists were Will Barnet, Angiola Churchill, Henry Finkelstein, and Jarrod Beck. The age of the four artists at the time of the interviews ranged from 35 to 101 years of age. While all four of the artists resided primarily in New York City, only one grew up in the city. Angiola and Henry often spent the summer months in Europe. Jarrod Beck spent much of his time out of the city working on his art at residencies across the country. He now lives in west Texas.

Theory of Interview Research

Once, I asked Dr. Anna Neumann (2010), who has conducted interview research for decades, why she made no indication of either approval or disapproval in relation to what an interviewee said. To this she emphatically replied, "Because it's not about me!" She continued, "By keeping silent now, I can tell a bigger story later." The story would be the story of the insight gained from more than one interview and what such interviews combined might say about people's thoughts on a subject of importance to her, the interviewer, to the interviewee, and to an audience of interested minds.

Luker (2008), in her text on relating to the social sciences as one does to salsa dancing, writes that "salsa-dancing sociologists do interviews in order to build theory" (p. 167). The interviews here served that very function. The hope was that within the interviews, there would be insights from which theory could be proposed on the development of artists and the roles of mentors and copying in that development.

Interview research involves gathering rich descriptions of people and their history or memory of it. It is a qualitative journey, not one of numbers, but of memories and hopes spoken. "Miles and Huberman (1994) argue that qualitative data, which are grounded in words rather than numbers, are a source of rich descriptions and explanations of processes" (Ardalan, 2009, p. 73). This is what the artists who participated in this study have provided: "rich descriptions and explanations" of their relationships with mentors and students and with copying and the artists who came before them.

Ardalan (2009) also notes that "Denzin and Lincoln (2003) suggest that qualitative research requires an intimate relationship between the researcher and what is studied" (p. 75). My relationship to the aims of this study is indeed intimate as I am an artist and have been a disciple and mentor. I care deeply about my field of art and do want to gain insight into how it is that aspiring artists become artists; how mentors shape lives; how disciples find mentors; what role copying in the broadest sense plays in this; and how the mind itself seeks mentors even from history.

Kvale (1996) says that "Interviews can be used to obtain descriptions of the cultural and the historical, the social and the material context of subjects' lives" (p. 293). I sought in the interview portion of this study to learn something of the role mentors have played in the lives of four artists, and perhaps from this small sample make inferences that could be helpful to future aspiring artists and their teachers who may become more like mentors.

Kvale also argues for interviewing outside of the office context and "in the subjects' natural surroundings, such as their workplace or home" (p. 293). This is what I have done. I interviewed two of the artists in their studios and the other two artists in their combined studio and home apartments. By interviewing the artists in their studios and homes, they felt a degree of comfort and I believe a greater sense of us as interviewer and interviewee as equals. I came with the goal of eliciting information according to an interview guide which related to my own study interest, but we were on their home turf, which thus hopefully allowed them greater comfort with its familiarity and fact that was their own. While the artists stayed focused on the questions asked, I derived greater insights into their work spaces, how they were arranged, and the amount of what appeared to me to be order or intentional disorder. Having some of their works and materials around illuminated the interviews and perhaps their own recollections and thus created an even richer source for gaining insights into thoughts and habits not spoken of, not asked of, undisclosed, covered, and revealed.

Neumann and Kvale both make clear that "the researcher's task [is] analyzing and constructing meaning" (Kvale, 1996, p. 180). The interviewee has the sole task of telling his or her story. In this fashion, I played the role of the questioner who listened, or the listener who prompted the direction of a conversation through questions. I tried not to judge. I did my best to suspend judgment and comments that conveyed judgment during the interview so that the interviewee could speak freely about what was most important and revealing about his relationship with his mentor or mentors.

> But that's exactly the point. I think that interviews are, almost by definition, accurate accounts of the kinds of mental maps that people carry around inside their heads, and that it is this, rather than some videotape of "reality," which is of interest to me.
>
> (Luker, 2008, p. 167)

What kinds of "mental maps" do artists carry in their minds? Like Luker, my interest was not so much in the specifics of times and dates, people and deeds, as much as it was in what the speaking of such implied about the thoughts of the artists. Is there a similar way that each went from young person to aspiring artist to artist? If so, what does that map look like? Is it the same or nearly so for each of the artists? Or is each map so personal so as to look nothing like the others', the other artists' maps to being?

I also sought to engage in a "phenomenological reduction," which Kvale (1996) describes as "a suspension of judgment as to the existence or nonexistence of the content of an experience ... in order to arrive at an unprejudiced description of the essence of the phenomena" (p. 84). Here, I believed the phenomena to be emotion, feelings of kinship, and concern for another and concern for an art form.

While an interview is considered to be a conversation and a conversation as a form of knowledge, I looked again to Kvale's (1996) text to describe the tradition of knowledge arising from conversation, just as Socrates sought to build in his students—disciples—knowledge through discourse. Kvale further notes that "in Rorty's neopragmatic philosopy, conversation is a basic mode of knowing" (p. 42), and I sought through this study to know more of the artists' development and the roles that mentors, copying, and historical mentors may have played in this.

Kvale (1996) describes the differing roles of the interviewees and the interviewer as storytellers to different audiences. The interviewees, in this case four artists, told their story to me, the interviewer (also an artist, though in this role, primarily a researcher of qualitative information). I then interpreted their stories and compared them to others' stories, and sought to tell a new story that included their stories and mine to another audience. The audience for this story may be readers of my dissertation or an audience of listeners at a presentation where I discuss the stories of the interviewees singularly, together, comparatively with each other, with myself, and against a historical record.

I also consider that in speaking to others, we are telling stories, which are not facts chronologically laid out but rather presentations of the experiences and interpretations of their effect and importance to others. Moreover, there are always the goals of the storyteller, goals known and not known to them, from which I as an interview researcher sought to draw meaning.

As an artist researching the relationship of disciples to their mentors in the development of artists, I brought to this study an element that Kvale (1996) argues is essential: "an expertise in the field studied, as a presupposition for arriving at valid interpretations" (p. 182). I am an artist and I have played the roles of disciple and mentor in my development and in the development of younger artists, and I have copied the work of the masters and modeled myself on the behavior and attitudes of my teachers and mentors.

Bourgault (2011) in her interview study of artists in the later decades of their lives speaks not only of the storytelling aspect of interviews and conversation in general, but of how when speaking of interviews and stories given, we as researchers are representing them, not giving them as they were given us.

> Given the philosophical consideration that every story is an interpretation carefully crafted through the agency of the storyteller, the researcher must take ownership of her own interpretation. The portraits that she will be creating from the conversations cannot be presented as the participants' stories but as her own representations. (p. 56)

To clarify further, what I made of what the artists in my study have said is logically my interpretation of their words spoken. Here, it is necessary to turn to Neumann's (1995) statement in her study about how resource stress within two colleges was constructed in part by those perceiving and speaking, or not perceiving and speaking, of it to others and how they did so. As she wrote, "My first-person voice is a reminder to the reader that what follows is my interpretation and thereby my construction, worked and reworked, of various college members' interpretations" (p. 6).

Thoughts on Autoethnography

Ellis (2004) considers autoethnography to be a research method which brings together personal, political, and social aspects, weaving them into one fabric, unlike the goals of the scientific method whereby the researcher seeks to stand outside the phenomena or history being studied. Ellis, Adams, and Bochner (2011) write of how it is that postmodern beliefs that came to the fore in the 1980s threw into doubt even the possibility that a researcher could be other than subjective. They speak of how it is that from this time of crisis in believing the objectivity of science and history, social scientists began to consider how their own work could be more like literature. They write,

> Gradually, scholars across a wide spectrum of disciplines began to consider what social sciences would become if they were closer to literature than to physics, if they proffered stories rather than theories, and if they were self-consciously value-centered rather than pretending to be value free. (p. 2)

In discussing his own autoethnographic study of his art making, Swift (2009) spoke of the need to combine multiple qualitative research methods to reach his goal of self-discovery with relevance to a larger audience that has interests in art, education, family, and the ways of learning what one has learned. He wrote:

> Thus, if qualitative methods from this tradition have done this and are a process void of the self, then to research the self would mean invention. The invention lies in the mixing or combining of methods drawn from traditional research methods focused on the other and turned on the self. (p. 109)

With autoethnography, there is a belief that the learning of the particular can have great value to the general; that one's story can be worth sharing and so enhance the lives of others. Hoelson and Burton (2012) wrote of their desire to share their conversations about their thoughts on the systematic changes in their country of South Africa with a more widely interested audience. They made no claims to advancing specific knowledge, but believed that

> [t]he primary aim of this autoethnographic study was to share and engage in scholarly conversation with interested others in a more public and critical context regarding our explorations and understanding of the nature and effects of specific spontaneous personal transformational moments that emerged in our dyadic dialogical conversation over time. (p. 94)

Ellis et al. (2011) spoke of autoethnography as being at times criticized by some social scientists as too literary and at the same time criticized by some autobiographical writers as too scientific. They argue that a goal of autoethnography is to combine the two forms of writing and so thought their work would bridge the unnecessary divide between science and art.

Autoethnography, as method, attempts to disrupt the binary of science and art. Autoethnographers believe research can be rigorous, theoretical, and analytical *and* emotional, therapeutic, and inclusive of personal and social phenomena. (p. 11)

In Supplement

In supplement to the interviews with the four artists, I phoned one to ask him follow-up questions, visited another to speak again in person, and wrote to and received e-mail responses from two others to specific questions about more simply answered questions such as the number of children in their family of origin or what their employment responsibilities included. Written materials such as books and exhibition catalogs were consulted largely for fact-checking and double-checking my own understandings as researcher of what the artists presented in the interviews. As an example, an interview with the painter Henry Finkelstein by the Jerusalem Studio School was available and I read it via the school's online archives. The reading of this interview added thoroughness to my own interview with him.

The artists' work was seen in exhibitions and in their work spaces and during studio visits. As mentioned previously, I knew the work of the four artists prior to beginning the study, although between the time the artists agreed to participate in the study to the final editing of the book, I was able to see more of their work in more places as they held exhibitions and created site-specific installations.

Treatment of Information

The interviews followed a general interview protocol and were transcribed and coded for patterns and places of similarity and dissimilarity, insights anew. The themes that emerged from the data within each transcript were considered in relation to the words of the other artists interviewed and in relation to artists of the past whose thoughts and history can be ascertained through artifacts, recorded interviews, and documents.

This information was needed to consider the nature of the relationship of the mentor to the disciple in the development of artists, if copying plays a role in that development, and if artists who were once mentored become mentors.

Organizing the Data

I listened to the interviews. I listened when we spoke. I thought the words and their meanings over in my mind. I listened when I transcribed the spoken word to written word. I listened more closely when I double- and triple-checked the transcriptions. During all this listening, I began to hear the artists' voices in my mind when reading their words or thinking about the time spent conversing. I made messy little charts on the backs of the interview protocols. I made more notes at the ends of the transcribed interviews. I spoke to my own artist colleagues about the study participant artists' words and what I heard in them.

After all the listening, I did some more reading of the transcriptions and so listened again to the voices of the artists in my mind, where sounds became meaning. During the reading and rereading of the transcripts, I would note in pencil on the transcripts areas of spoken, now written, words that related to the research questions. I noted things that were agreeing or disagreeing with what others had said. Places of common experience received the greatest attention. Places of discussion of mentors, masters, copying, and student disciples were considered over and over and in relation to what I recalled the other participants saying or not saying.

My memory and notes were the primary instruments of organizing the data, just as my person and voice were the primary instruments of gathering the data with the help of a digital voice recorder and word processor later. Maughan (2006) in discussing the characteristics of qualitative research wrote that "In qualitative research, the researcher becomes the primary instrument for collecting data" (p. 118). So I was.

This was a mind game. The game I played in my mind was to make some sense of place and purpose to what each had said and consider it in relation to my own experience and the art history I have read. I took a break of days or weeks to see where it would continue to thread into the next and the next, if at all. Writing is a thinking game, and this thinking of what was said is part and way of that game. By thinking game, I mean sense-making and theory-building behaviors of mind. The written words here are explanations of my thoughts for others. So this was my method.

References

Ardalan, S. (2009). *Apprenticeship in the arts and crafts of Iran: The mentorship practices of four masters.* Unpublished dissertation, EdD, Teachers College, Columbia University, New York, NY.

Bourgault, R. (2011). *Retrospections and interpretations: The narrative of ageing artists on the complexities of their creative practices through time.* Unpublished dissertation, EdD, Teachers College, Columbia University, New York, NY.

Buber, M. (1958). *I and thou* (2nd ed.) (R. G. Smith, trans.). New York, NY: Charles Scribner's Sons.

Ellis, C. (2004). *The ethnographic I: A methodological novel about autoethnography.* Walnut Creek, CA: AltaMira Press.

Ellis, C., Adams, T. E., & Bochner, A. P. (2011). Autoethnography: An overview. *Forum Qualitative Sozialforschung/Forum: Qualitative Social Research, 12*(1), Art. 10.

Hoelson, C. N., & Burton, R. (2012). Conversing life: An autoethnographic construction. *The Qualitative Report, 17*(1), 92–119.

Kvale, S. (1996). *Interviews: An introduction to qualitative research interviewing.* San Francisco, CA: Sage.

Luker, K. (2008). *Salsa dancing into the social sciences: Research in the age of infoglut.* Cambridge, MA: Harvard University Press.

Maughan, B. D. (2006). *Mentoring among scientists: Implications of interpersonal relationships within a formal mentoring program.* Albuquerque, NM: Winter Meeting and Nuclear Technology Expo.

Maxwell, J. A. (1992). *Qualitative research design: An interactive approach.* Los Angeles, CA: Sage.

Neuman, A. (1995). On the making of hard times and good times: The social construction of resource stress. *The Journal of Higher Education, 66*(1), 3–31.

Neumann, A. (2010). *Class lectures in "The craft of interview research".* New York, NY: Teachers College, Columbia University.

Swift, J. (2009). *Reflective inquiry and artistic practice: Identifying consistencies originating from experience.* Unpublished EdD doctoral dissertation, Teachers College, Columbia University, New York, NY.

5   Four Artists on Mentors

Introduction

In this chapter, I discuss the process of the interview research and what was found, discuss the main themes that arose during the interviews with the four artists and possible reasons for them, and discuss the concept of mentors in our minds and mentoring as human nurturance.

When and Where

I spoke with Will Barnet at his studio in New York City in the spring of 2012. I spoke with Angiola Churchill at her home and studio, as they are one space divided into living and workspaces, also in New York City. We spoke in the late winter. Henry Finkelstein and I spoke at his studio in Long Island City that same season. Long Island City is just east of Manhattan on the most western part of Queens, which is a borough of New York City. In the cold winds of Provincetown, Massachusetts, on a sunny winter day, I walked the beach with Jarrod Beck before we went to his small apartment at the Provincetown Work Space, where he was nearing the end of a nine-month artist's residency. We visited his studio just next door before we began the interview.

How

The how of how I came to be privileged to speak with these four artists was simply the act of asking and knowing. I asked three of the four via an e-mail invitation, in which I briefly discussed the purpose of the study and their potential role in it as a subject to be interviewed. These three artists—Angiola Churchill, Henry Finkelstein, and Jarrod Beck—I had known prior to the study in some professional fashion. I respect and admire their work, and Henry and Jarrod have expressed the same regard for my drawings and paintings. They each let me know they would gladly participate and we from there worked out the when and where.

DOI: 10.4324/9781003451303-5

Will Barnet, I did not know other than as a figure from history and a man whom I saw visiting Robert Blackburn (Bob) at his print shop on West 17th Street in New York City. Between 1988 and 1990, I worked there on my etchings and lithographs through Bob's graciousness because I had no money to pay for renting the time but rather earned it by helping to teach classes to adults and children. Mr. Barnet, I recall, visited Bob regularly. They spoke as old friends, I could tell from a distance.

Some decades later when Dr. Judith Burton and I were speaking, she mentioned that she had briefly spoken with Will Barnet at a recent gala event for the Rutgers University Center for Innovative Print and Paper. We both thought at almost what seemed the same moment that he would make an invaluable contribution to the study. I forthwith wrote him a letter describing all that I relayed above and the purpose of the study and mailed it to his attention to the National Academy Museum in New York City, which had only a few months before held a large exhibition of his work to celebrate his 100th birthday. I saw that exhibition on December 31, 2011.

Whom

I here write of the biographical and educational history of the four artists with whom I spoke in brief terms. This information came to me through their words in our discussions and was further solidified in my reading of their biographies and exhibition catalogs.

Will Barnet

Will Barnet, born in 1911, grew up in "you know, the usual family." That was in Beverly, Massachusetts. His first artistic undertakings, he told me, came when he was a boy of about 12 and found a book on the French artist Honore Daumier at the Beverly Public Library (Figure 5.1). He was so taken with the reproductions of the artist's drawings that he copied them. At the same place of study, he read the four volumes of *The History of Art* by the French scholar Elie Faure at around the tender age of 14: "So that was a very influential book. I spent a long time reading four volumes."

Mr. Barnet then studied at the School of the Museum of Fine Arts in Boston in the "great French tradition" under the direction of the painter Philip Hale: "I spent a year working from great Greek casts drawing." Then, "I had life drawing for a year." He got a bit restless and applied to the Art Students League in New York City where he was accepted and received a full four-year scholarship.

In his first year at the League, he chose to study with the painter Stuart Davis. Mr. Barnet remembers Jackson Pollock as beginning at the League at the same time (Jackson Pollock chose to study with Thomas Hart Benton). Of

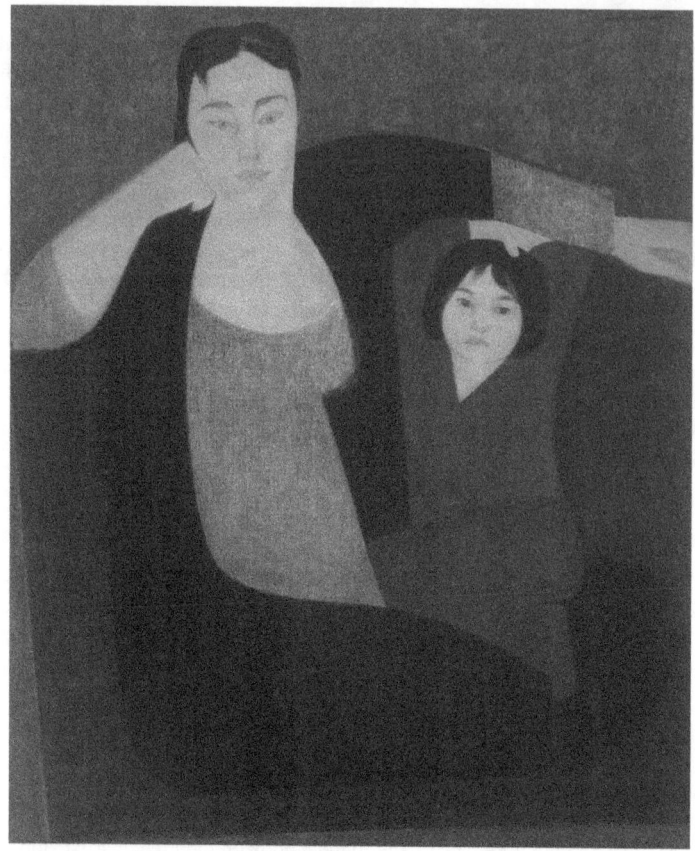

Figure 5.1 Will Barnet. *Mother and Child*, 1961 (oil on canvas, 46 × 39 inches).
© The Estate of Will Barnet, courtesy Alexandre Gallery, New York.

Stuart Davis, Mr. Barnet said, "And I like Davis' work, so perhaps that was the closest to being a mentor to me, a live mentor." Yet when asked why that was so, he said, "Well, he wasn't really a mentor in the sense of being very personable with me, spending time and so forth. He was a man who came in and taught to the general group of students who were there."

Mr. Barnet learned lithography while a student at the League, and in a short time, he came to be the printer for the League, making prints of artists' etchings or lithographs and the like. He then became an instructor of print-making and painting while at the League where he taught for 47 years. He also taught painting at The Cooper Union in New York City for about 35 years and at the Pennsylvania Academy of Fine Arts in Philadelphia for nearly the same time. "So I taught simultaneously at The League, The Cooper Union, and The Pennsylvania Academy at the same time. Three schools at the same time." During the summer months, he traveled to other universities and taught a class titled "Putting the World Together."

Angiola Churchill

Angiola was a professor of a class of mine some decade earlier at Teachers College and we stayed in touch primarily through occasional visits I made to her home, largely to discuss her work and what she was up to in showing her work, which meant installing labyrinths and paper gardens in spaces around Europe (Figure 5.2).

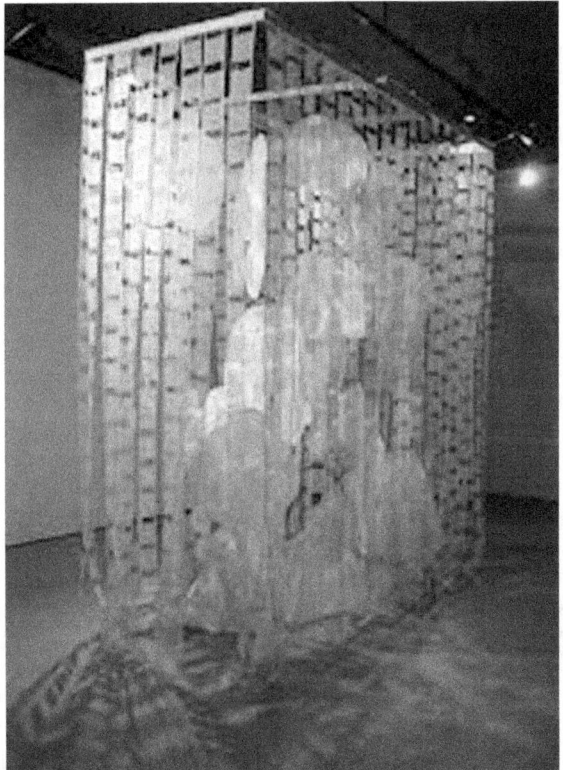

Figure 5.2 Angiola Churchill. Installation view of one section of *Oltre Il Giardino*, 2003 (paper).

The Museo Fortuny, Venice, Italy.

Angiola will readily say that she had a "very privileged life." But in fact, I think it was as difficult as it was privileged, or perhaps just a life. By privileged, she meant she was born into a large, well-established, and respected Italian family with long roots in the region of Italy where she grew up. I point out the difficulty she described as being sickly as an infant and although she was born in New York City, her mother's doctor suggested she take Angiola back to Italy as she was not nursing and growing strong, but rather weaker and weaker.

This her mother did, which meant a week or two on a boat across an ocean without her husband, Angiola's father, who stayed in New York where he was the owner of a restaurant. The privilege of wealth allowed Angiola's mother to take her from Italy to Switzerland where they were developing baby formulas. This seems to have saved her life in infancy.

Another story Angiola told me of her childhood was that her legs were somehow deformed and there seemed to be no cure for that either, but the older women of her family's village would get the hot fat from the butcher every day and massaged her legs with it. It seemed the hot fat and massaging worked, Angiola is in her late 90s.

Angiola does not ascribe her development as an artist to anyone. She does ascribe it to everyone—to everyone she grew up with and around who encouraged her to draw, paint, or make things and to everyone at the High School of Music and Art in New York City who were her teachers because "They were all great!" She does ascribe her intellectual growth and historical understanding to many—to the many expatriate Italians who came to her father's home in New York City and his farm upstate during the horrors of Fascist Italy before World War II (how "I learned about the whole world from them!"). From the many artists on 8th Street whom she observed as an 18-year-old young woman, she learned what she did not want. She learned that she did not want to be an artist's wife because it seemed to her that male artists "just got drunk all day and then yelled at their wives who were going out working."

Mentors? Not for Angiola Riva Churchill! No, not as an artist. As an artist, Angiola is a force of nature and she has aspired to create new, and she has. She was born deeply immersed in the living history of Italy in a region that had been the center of an arts-based economy for centuries. "Everybody drew! That's what they did, for centuries! That's the kind of place I grew up in!"

But as an art educator, as one who worked with children and then became the first woman professor at New York University's School of Art and later its chair for 12 years, she had a mentor: Victor D'Amico, a renowned art educator who was the director of the Museum of Modern Art's education department and who guided her into the modern world of art from the centuries of Italian art to which she was born. Her teachers at Music and Art High School chose her to participate in the Young People's Gallery which D'Amico had established at the museum.

He brought her into the job she loved most her whole life: teaching children at The Ethical Culture School in New York City. It was D'Amico again who insisted that she give up Ethical Culture and working with children to teach at the university.

Henry Finkelstein

Henry Finkelstein paints landscapes from observation outdoors, trying to capture sensory impressions of light, color, and movement with the plastic medium of pigment immersed in oils placed upon a canvas surface. He also draws the same with graphite on paper and begins his oil paintings with light, drawing upon its surface. During the winter months when painting landscapes outdoors is far more difficult because of the weather and because he is living in New York City during that time, he paints still-life and works on landscape paintings begun earlier in nature (Figure 5.3).

He seems to have been born to be a painter. In fact, he is embarrassed that he never thought of anything else to do. "It's kind of embarrassing," he said, about never having considered any other profession or life.

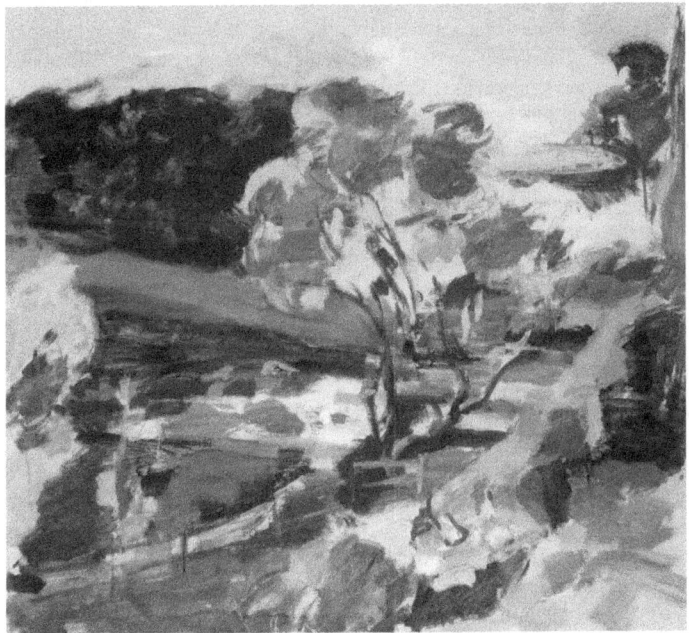

Figure 5.3 Henry Finkelstein. *Scene Along the Trieux*, 2023 (oil on canvas, 48 × 54).

Henry grew up in New York City and was reared as almost an only child as his sister was 12 years older. Both parents were painters and teachers: Greta Campbell and Louis Finkelstein. He said it was "the only thing that was valued in the house." At around age 10, he would walk across Central Park from the West Side where he lived to the Metropolitan Museum of Art, where he would go and draw in front of the paintings of Poussin: "Kind of a strange thing to do for a kid."

He went from high school to study at The Cooper Union and then from there to continue studying at The Yale School of Art to earn a master's degree, which he stated he did largely because of an erroneous concern about being drafted into the military were he not in school. From Yale, Henry went to Italy on a Fulbright Fellowship to study the masters of the Italian Renaissance.

Through the son I came to know of the parents, their work, and their public history. Henry seems to have closely followed his parents' footsteps. His father also attended The Cooper Union and while not a student at Yale, was a professor there. In painting style also, it appears, perhaps superficially, in means: painting landscapes from observation out in the world. His mother Greta Campbell also painted from observation landscapes and taught painting at Yale.

Henry agreed to join in the study and speak of his mentors. The primary mentor was Ruben Kadish, whom he met as a student at The Cooper Union. He mentions my own painting teacher who taught him some seven years before, Nicholas Marsicano. He also mentions Lester Young later being a positive force at The Yale School of Art. He never told me directly that both his parents painted landscapes from observation just as he does. He finds drawing and painting outdoors the most invigorating way of working. On a number of occasions, he mentioned how he finds the winter so hard because that is when he works in the studio on still-life paintings that do not hold the excitement of working outdoors in the sun, wind, and shade of France and Maine.

Henry teaches part-time at two New York institutions: the Art Students League, where Will Barnet taught, and the National Academy of Art, where he is a national academician, as is Will Barnet. National academicians are chosen by their peers to the honor in an effort to recognize and preserve the works of great American artists.

Jarrod Beck

Jarrod Beck takes the materials he finds and seeks in the world and turns them into something, what every artist does, although Jarrod has been using more industrial found, and self-processed trees and such materials. He creates spaces of vast interest. Some would call them installations. Some would call them sculptures. Other works might be called process art as he invites the public to witness the building and creating of some of the spaces. He also draws and makes prints and sometimes turns those prints into sculptures. Plaster, wood, and burnt materials are loved media (Figure 5.4).

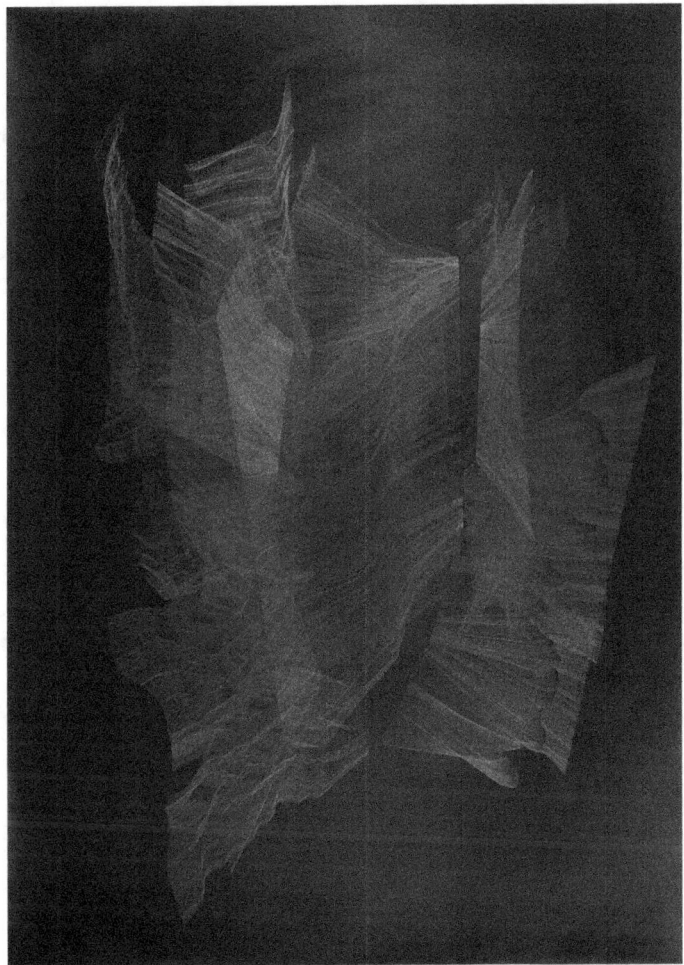

Figure 5.4 Jarrod Beck. Cinerum, 2012 (Graphite and Charcoal on paper, 40 × 60).
Photo credit: Paul Takeuchi.

Jarrod studied architecture at Tulane University as a young man. He chose to be an artist and then pursued further study at the University of Texas in Austin where he focused on creating installations. His MFA degree is in studio art from that university. I met him at the Vermont Studio Center where I was a resident for a month and he was visiting a friend who was also a resident. We met and found things to talk about.

He grew up in New York State primarily alone with his mother as his parents were divorced. Jarrod remembers always being encouraged to draw and finding great pleasure in doing so, especially when a loved one or admired and caring teacher found beauty in his work. His teachers seemed to have been of great importance to him, and as mentors were the subject of our discussions, which may, in part, explain the fond memories he shared with me about them.

Jarrod lives in West Texas now and works on his art in many other places as opportunities and artist residencies are offered to him. He has worked at the Fine Arts Work Center in Provincetown, MA, the Taliesin Artist Residency of the Frank Lloyd Wright School of Architecture in Arizona and Wisconsin, and the Socrates Sculpture Park in Long Island City, Queens, NY.

For four years, he worked full-time at the Guggenheim Museum's design installation department. His "job was to translate a curator's research into a design approach for the exhibition." He continues to do this now as a consultant. He pursues his art and opportunities to make work in public or open to the public spaces with vigor.

Main Themes

There are the four areas around which questions and follow-up questions were designed and then asked of the four artists participating in this study. These areas were designed to solicit responses from the participants that might contribute to answering the research questions on mentoring and copying in the development of artists. They are Mentors in Your Development, Copying, Mentors in Your Mind, and Mentors to Others.

Mentors in Your Development

Speaking in Riddles

Sometimes the mentors of the artists of the study spoke in riddles or they did not speak at all directly, and the disciple learned by looking, reflecting, and aspiring. Like Kadish, Henry said that "Marsicano spoke in riddles too, I think." The challenges that a mentor issues a disciple are frequently not direct. They are more like riddles that one can think upon for a lifetime, not a recipe to follow from here to there.

The Number One Mentor

The number one mentor for Angiola Churchill was the greatly respected art education advocate Victor D'Amico, who in the mid-1930s was working at the Museum of Modern Art's education department and became a national figure and advocate for art education that championed children creating from imagination and exploratory engagement rather than learning forms and manners from rote.

Angiola came into his orbit of influence when she was selected by her teachers at the High School of Music and Art in New York City to participate in a program for high school students at the Museum of Modern Art called The Young People's Gallery. It was directed by D'Amico with the aim of having high school students curate an exhibition of modern art using the museum's collection and installing it in one of the museum's galleries. She was a high school girl and although D'Amico was not teaching the class, she remembers him watching it from a distance.

I remember the first days I went to MOMA, and Victor D'Amico would sit on the side there. He would sit there and watch while somebody else taught the class.

Though Angiola has pooh-poohed this study in her words, although not in her deeds by participating, she did adamantly say some many hours into our discussions:

Listen, D'Amico saw me as a child, I mean I was a kid. He never forgot about me. He was always my mentor. D'Amico. If anybody was my mentor, it was D'Amico.

D'Amico seems to have played a large role in Angiola's career as an art educator: inviting her to be part of the Museum of Modern Art's many committees to lay out the values of art education for children and teens, appreciating her teaching at the elementary level of The Ethical Culture School where D'Amico was in charge of the high school, and directly advocating for her to become a part of the faculty at New York University. He seems to have always been there guiding, advocating, and arguing with Angiola since she entered his life. She said of their mentor and disciple relationship:

We fought like cats and dogs, because he, I don't why, because. Because he was always wanting to be in charge and I was always escaping. But he had his eye on me since I was in high school. He knew me since I was in high school.

She built on D'Amico's importance to her nearly 50-year career as an art educator at the elementary and university level by saying, "But I owe D'Amico a lot. Even though I wasn't aware of it, he was doing things for me." While Angiola was chosen for this study because of her work as an artist, the greatest mentor in her professional life was in art education. Yet, it is through art education that one can become more of an artist and learn part of the craft, history, and philosophy.

Having grown up in and been surrounded by the rich living history of Renaissance craft and ironworks in Italy, Angiola developed a strong bias toward it. She said of modern art, "All right, so what happened was that I, I didn't like modern art. I liked art of the Renaissance. I liked all that stuff." She found herself in New York City at the Museum of Modern Art with a group of young people charged with selecting works of modern art to exhibit for the general public who came to the museum. This was an education, set up in large part by D'Amico, and so Angiola came to appreciate that which she did not. She said of that time, "I remember I didn't like this stuff. I thought it wasn't much good, or whatever it was. So it was quite an education."

Henry Finkelstein's number one mentor—the one he wanted to speak to me most about, I believe, to honor him—was Ruben Kadish. He described Kadish as more of an art philosopher than a professor of drawing, painting, or sculpture. To my knowledge, Ruben Kadish did not have the college or university degrees that such places now require before they even consider hiring anyone to teach what one knows. Henry told me that he took classes with Kadish just "to hang out near him," not because he expected to learn anything about sculpture or drawing—the titles of classes that Kadish taught.

To the question I posed Henry, "Did you have him for a particular class?" he responded:

I had him…he was like a philosophy teacher of art. I mean I had him, I took sculpture with him, but it was just an excuse to hang out near him. I couldn't do sculpture to save my life. And he was allowed to teach a drawing class and we just drew the figure and he just sat there and talked. He didn't really critique your drawings per se, at all I don't think.

It was the energy, philosophy, and wisdom of Ruben Kadish that seemed to have attracted Henry to him and that remains in his memory today. No instruction about building forms or shading masses was given. They had discussions of beliefs such as an artist having something to say beyond just being a "watered-down version" of someone else. Henry said that "One of the things he talked about that I thought was true newness, was the pedigree, his idea of the pedigree." When I asked Henry what Kadish meant by the term, he said:

But the idea of pedigree. The idea of "Like what are you doing that no one else is doing?" You know, ok, you're influenced by this, this, and this, but what are you doing with it? Or are you just a watered-down little less than it? And no one had ever said that to me before.

Henry remembered that for the rest of his life. He asks himself what is he doing with his passion for the paintings of Titian, Bonnard, and Poussin that honors them but is different from them. He asked himself what he was doing that was different from what his parents did—both of whom were painters and so were his first painting teachers in addition to his first teachers in life.

Jarrod spoke of Javier as having the most profound effect on him. Javier was his first architecture professor in undergraduate school and also a painter. He seems to have demonstrated for Jarrod a way of being in the world as an artist and as a man, although his assigned role was architecture professor. Jarrod saw in him opportunities for ways of being in this world of people, society. When I asked Jarrod, "What did he role model?" Jarrod said,

> You know, he was someone who was comfortable with who he was and maybe that was how he was a role model to me because I did not feel that at the time, I felt like I was very unsure of myself, and definitely unsure of myself as a gay man. So, he just encouraged me to maybe take some chances socially.

Later on, I asked Jarrod, "Have you considered yourself a disciple to anyone?" He said he had felt he was a disciple to Javier and that others had seen him that way also, saying:

> I think when I was eighteen and a student of Javier's I got a feeling like I was a disciple of his. I took a lot of his studios. I think other people saw me as a disciple of his.

Will Barnet's number one mentors were the painters from history whom he admired: "They were my mentors." The men with whom he studied in the early 1930s at the Boston Museum School and then at the Art Students League were good men who did their job of teaching drawing and painting concepts well but who were not very personable toward him or the other students. He said to me, "Instructors at that time were very different than today."

"It Was a Vote of Confidence"

When his college professor asked him to work on an architectural project outside of the school, Jarrod said, "It was a vote of confidence." Of the same professor he said that his first impression of him was "he could be very closed off. I remember seeing him for the first time and thinking 'He wanted nothing to do with any of us.'"

Jarrod recalled the same feeling when later on in graduate school, another professor sought his help little by little, with increasing responsibility and trust each time. First, she asked him to watch her home and care for her cats during the summer when she was away. Jarrod took this, and logically so, as an indication of her trust in him. In return for his home and feline caring, Jarrod received not only validation and a larger social and professional relationship with his professor whom he described as a mentor, but he also had the benefit of being able to use her studio and enjoy her large collection of books and other art resources.

Later on and to this day, she acts as a mentor to him in that she built her career, in part, by traveling and working at artists' residencies. Jarrod was in a nine-month residency at the time of this interview and said that, in part, both she and his mentor/professor from undergraduate school "modeled" for him ways to participate in the art world through projects and residencies.

> I think from Javier's influence, also, I think Margot's, I have continued to travel and to create situations where I continue to travel and can create new things and let that be an influence in my work.

Henry mentioned a similar feeling of no longer being invisible and of being seen as someone with some worth when the man whom he describes as his mentor recognized him.

> It felt very rewarding when Kadish finally seemed to appreciate me and not think I was, and think I was bright. You know, you didn't always know if he liked you. He was kind of like Saint Jerome. He was kind of like a grumpy old man.

So when Kadish recognized Henry, Henry felt valued and understood that Kadish valued what he was doing and how he was thinking. This was important to Henry. When Javier and then Margot invited Jarrod to work with them outside of the university, he felt valued, that he was more than just "a sincere and polite student."

Will Barnet mentioned no such moment when he felt valued by a mentor or professor who had previously seemed uninterested. When I asked him if he had kept in touch with Philip Hale, his drawing instructor at the Boston Museum School, he said:

> No. We, I had a very friendly relationship with him, but instructors at that time were very different than today. Sometimes they're more intimate with their students. But he was very friendly and very good and he gave me advice on what to do when I got to New York.

He studied with the great American painter Stuart Davis for one year at the Art Students League. "But unfortunately, Davis didn't teach too long there, so I lost him as a teacher." He did mention that Davis was "the closest to being a mentor to me, a live mentor." When I asked him why that was, he said:

> Well, he wasn't really a mentor in the sense of being very personable with me spending time and so forth. He was a man who came in and taught to the general group of students who were there.

While Angiola mentioned how her mentor Victor D'Amico "had his eye on me since I was in high school. He knew me since I was in high school," she never mentioned a particular moment when she went from feeling inconsequential to him, then feeling noticed. Rather, D'Amico seems to have noticed her from the beginning, but she did not care one way or the other whether he did.

Visiting the Mentor at Home

Both Henry and Jarrod visited the homes and work spaces of their mentors at their mentors' invitations. These invitations to the private beyond the institution of the college and university further shifted the relationship from one of teacher and student to mentor and disciple. Students do not go to professors' homes; students go to class. Teachers teach in classes in schools. Mentors teach all the time, and mostly when they are not officially teaching, but always through word, instruction, and insights given.

Henry said of his most influential mentor Ruben Kadish that when he went to his home,

> he didn't change really from teaching. He just talked about these things that I knew there was wisdom behind them. I would walk away and still think about them a bit.

Henry was first invited to Kadish's home along with other students at Kadish's invitation to a picnic. Later on, Henry would drop in seeing Kadish on his own. When I first asked Henry if he ever visited any of his mentors at their homes, he said,

> But, Kadish yeah. I don't know if you ever did, but he would have these picnics out in New Jersey out on his farm and it was really nice. He would invite a whole bunch of students and other artists that he knew. He was pretty gregarious that way. Sometimes, I remember after Cooper Union, and being at his house in New York. Just dropping in, I'm not sure why.

Jarrod spent long periods of time at his mentor Margot's home in Texas in the capacity of cat- and home-sitter while she was away during the summer, and that grew to the capacity of an assistant on a large public commission. Of the times at Margot's home and studio, Jarrod said:

> I always felt like when I would drive to her studio and her house, the same building, and that was thirty minutes outside Austin. I felt this immense sense of relief. Because I would, I could become myself again and just work and eat and live and, you know, go through all these emotions within this very positive and creative environment.

Will Barnet never mentioned visiting any of his teachers at their homes. As quoted earlier, he did say, "Instructors at that time were very different than today. Sometimes they're more intimate with their students." His mentors were the old masters.

Copying Works of Art or the Mentor's Ways

Copying

Who copied? Will Barnet copied the drawings of Honore Daumier that he admired from a book in the local public library when he was a boy of 14 or so. He also learned to draw the figure by copying plaster casts. He did this for a full year under the guidance of his teacher, the artist Philip Hale at the School of the Museum of Fine Arts in Boston in 1929. Although he constantly studied the work of Ingres and other great French masters, his actual copying seems limited to two artists: "The two artists I copied were Daumier and El Greco." The paintings of El Greco that Will Barnet copied were for his "thesis of study at the Boston Museum.... I made a copy of a painting that they have at the Museum. A beautiful painting."

When I asked Will Barnet why he copied the work of Daumier as a young teen, he replied, "Well, I wanted to find a way of, the art of composing figures together and in groups like the Daumier." He discussed how he found Daumier's work to possess a structure he wanted in his own work. He built upon this by saying, "And the power of his drawings, they're not just drawings, but they're like a piece of sculpture almost. They have that feeling."

He further discussed the artists from history whom he looked to and studied, and spoke of Ingres, Chardin, Poussin, Giotto, and other "early Italian artists." He found their paintings "structurally sound and exciting and intense" and said of himself, "But I didn't know how to do it. So I had to copy someone and I should be able to understand how to do it for myself, the way I wanted."

Angiola Churchill first said that she never copied when asked: "I never really did, no. I wasn't one for copying other people's work." But then she did remember, "except for one time, I think for myself," copying the paintings of an Italian Baroque artist, whose name she could not remember at that moment, to learn about gardens. She "was very interested to find out how it might have felt to be in that place," and so she made "three or four large paintings based on that" painting. Thus, Angiola copied a painting to figure out what it might have felt like to be somewhere else and to learn about Archaic gardens. The painting, she later remembered, was by Raphael.

Angiola discussed her teaching and mentioned that she had one group of fine arts students from New York University and they were visiting a palace in Venice that had paintings by "the great Venetian painter" Titian. The students, "they could just go through and no one stopped or did anything and they were a little bit bored. I was so incensed!" And so, Angiola said to them:

> We're going in again and each one of you is going to choose a painting and you're going to stay in front of it for three hours! And you're going to write, or do anything.

The next day they did return and all chose a painting to stay in front of for three hours—and so did Angiola.

> For three hours, I stayed in front of that painting, and I got to know it. They still have it in the Academia and I can see it any time I want to. It was a painting that he did when he was an old man. And why I chose that one, it had no color at all. And I stayed in front of that painting for three hours like they did. And I thought I'd sweat myself to tears!

Angiola did not direct her students to copy the painting by drawing it, though some may have in the time they spent with it. Angiola herself did not mention drawing the Titian she stood in front of for three hours, but she did say:

> I know I got something out of it. They must have gotten something from sitting in front of something for three hours. They must have looked at it in some way. And I suppose they were cursing me. I was cursing them. But these are my great adventures in studying art.

At a later discussion, Angiola told me of how she occasionally taught studio classes at NYU, although she was hired for the art education department. One such class was an advanced painting class in which she would project a great painting upon the wall of the studio, and the students would then as a group draw out the basic figures and composition and go about painting it. Of the students and her own feelings about making a mural-size painting during the course of one class as an attempt to learn something about painting by painting the work of a master, she exclaimed, "What an exhilarating experience!"

The Raft of the Medusa by Théodore Géricault that now hangs in the grand room of French painting in the Louvre is one such painting that Angiola projected upon a massive paper for her students. She described the method and feeling of fatigue and exhilaration:

> No, we would project the size of it. And everybody would draw it. Would draw it like crazy because it was on the thing. Would step back and two hours later we were dead tired and full of pain and whatnot and we would look at the painting and we had done this great painting. What an exhilarating experience! It gives you a sense of power. It gives you a sense of your own power and what you can do.

When I asked her if they painted every week based upon a historical painting, she said, "That's what they did every week because they were learning things." She also spoke of how she would take three or four actual paintings from NYU's collection to the class and she specifically directed her students.

And I would say, "Pick something that you have a real affinity for. One of these guys. One of these four guys. These four great paintings, you have an affinity for. And paint a painting for the next three hours that is off of this painting, anything that you can think about."

Henry Finkelstein told me, "I think I copied Poussin when I was ten." He walked across Central Park in New York City from his parents' home on the Upper West Side to the Metropolitan Museum of Art. "Kind of a funny thing for a kid to do, huh?" he commented.

Henry copied the drawings and paintings of the great masters to learn from them, to look at them more closely, and to own them in a new way. Of the time he spent in Italy on a Fulbright scholarship, he said:

I lived in Italy for a year and I went around and copied things all the time: sculptures, paintings. What it did for me is it kind of fixed it in my memory. I had to slow down my eye and I had an experience.

Through copying, Henry felt that he came to "own" the painting. "I can still remember the experience of copying a Duccio. I own that Duccio for myself. For all time." By copying, Henry felt that the work of centuries past became present for him: "It made me appreciate the Duccio, which until I saw it, a thirteenth century painting, it wasn't anything I would have felt in the present tense."

Henry copied the works of many other great Italian Renaissance artists: "I copied Donatello. I copied Giovanni Pisano, Bolero, Michelangelo, The Medici Tombs...." Copying made these works permanent for him: "And through that year in Italy it fixed things in my mind."

Jarrod Beck never copied the works of other artists. His initial college training was as an architect and his master's training was in studio art with a focus on environmental art, printmaking, and creating spaces and installations. This did not mean he could not copy the work of others, but he did not. Nor did he seek to own a painting as Henry did, to learn about a garden as Angiola did, or to learn to draw as Will Barnet did when copying Daumier's drawings.

How Mentors Showed Ways to Be

After all the responses of "No" that Jarrod gave to my questions about ever copying the work of another artist, he did tell me "Yes" when I asked if he ever copied any of his mentors' "ways of being in the world." To this, he answered affirmatively.

> Well, I think from Javier's influence, also, I think Margot's, I have continued to travel and to create situations where I continue to travel and can create new things and let that be an influence in my work.

And what is the role model? Jarrod spoke of how it was from his college professor Javier's lived example of being both an architect and a painter that he felt "I knew in my deep down that it was ok that I did not become an architect who worked in an office." He saw in his architecture teacher another way "that I could be, that I could kind of expand my ways of being creative and kind of following the path of an artist."

From Margot, a graduate school professor whom Jarrod described as another mentor, he saw a way to be an artist in the world. He saw things that artists do such as go on residencies and make art.

> And Margot, and Margot. Yeah, I'm on a residency now and Margot was very encouraging. She's a very successful artist and she's been on a lot of residencies so I think hearing about all of those kind of encouraged me to try and get one of these residencies for myself.

Margot's success as an artist for Jarrod made going on residencies one of the ways to success.

Ruben Kadish showed or modeled for Henry a way of relating to art that was aspiring to be among the greatest artists, to be more than "just a watered-down version of something else." He talked about how Kadish used the term "pedigree" to refer to what an artist is going to contribute to the world, to the tradition and history of art of which they are partaking.

> Which meant that what you do should be the first of its kind. Should not be just a watered-down version of something else. But he didn't have any pretense that meant it should be like, a new theory of physics or a new, a new, medium that's never been seen before. It could, obviously it would have to include, he didn't go into it, but it would have to include things of the past. A culture. It would have to include culture, but he was kind of anti culture in a way, he was kind of Rousseauian.

What this meant for Henry was to ask of himself without denying the influence of and interest in other artists: "What are you doing that no one else is doing?" He continued speaking of Kadish's intent: "Ok, you're influenced by this, this, and this, but what are you doing with it? Or are you just watered-down little less than it?" Again, mentors challenge.

Having studied with Ruben Kadish myself in two courses and having been a close friend with someone who spent much time with him, I can say that Kadish cared about art. He cared about people making great things that had inherent valuable qualities in themselves and would contribute and build upon the greatest human achievements thus far and before. My friend Robyn Love once came to me and said, "Kadish asked, 'Do you want to make work for Soho or for the Louvre?'" Soho at that time was a part of Manhattan with many contemporary art galleries and many persons selling works to eager collectors. Of course, the work had to be what the collectors wanted. The challenge was to disregard the temptation of immediate financial reward and fame for lasting qualities that could stand the test of time and so merit inclusion in the greatest of museums, the Louvre.

Nicholas Marsicano, Henry's painting teacher at The Cooper Union and later mine, set an example for Henry of how to think of all painting as connected and how the value of a work of Titian from the 16th century could be considered in the same thought as the work of 20th-century artists.

> Marsicano kind of wove the whole tradition together, like he would talk about Titian and de Kooning in the same phrase. He made the whole tradition alive and present. Which was a wonderful thing. Kind of a rare thing!

Mentors in Our Minds

Those we aspire to be like, to make work like, say to us from history and the history of our seeing their works, "You can do things this way" or "Does it have the luminosity?" or "But what about the passion?" The mentors in our minds are those great artists from history whom we know by their work, only we did not have the opportunity to study with them and hear their voices in person. We choose to model ourselves or some part of our art on their work. They are in our minds through desire and seeking and holding dear.

Henry Finkelstein's mentors from the history of painting were Titian—"The greatest"—and Bonnard—"No! Bonnard, I love the work as much as Titian. The way he uses color as a metaphor. He's very important to me." He told me about the importance of the great artists of the past whom he studied by making copies of their work: "Oh! At my age I feel fortunate to just kind of have them in my veins and not really think about much when I paint." Thus, while Henry thinks about the great paintings and painters of the past, he does not do so while he is in the act of painting. They are so much a part of him that he need not.

Jarrod compares his work to that of the architect Louie Kahn when he asks himself if an installation is finished:

> There are moments when I'm in an installation I've built or created and I think, I might think of some detail, or some quality of light that is present in the Louie Kahn building that I've witnessed.

Jarrod also spoke of the effect of the artist David Wojnarowicz, whose way of being "brutally honest" in his journals encouraged Jarrod to try being as unafraid of offending others' sensibilities in his own writing. When describing to me how David Wojnarowicz enters his thoughts when he is working, he said:

> Like recently I started grappling with a relationship in my past that I kind of wanted to write about and build into an installation eventually. And I felt that. In reading David's journal entries, I....David is just there. I mean his personal journals he probably had an idea that they would be published in the future. He's just very ah, (sigh) he's just so brutally honest about what he's going through, about what he's feeling, that I think I try to bring some of that into writing.

The masters of European painting were Will Barnet's mentors from the past, those almost always in his mind. Above his desk in his studio hang postcards of paintings by Ingres, Vermeer, and El Greco. Stavitsky (2000) writes about how Barnet's instructor at the Boston Museum School, Philip Hale

> wrote a book on Vermeer (1913) that made quite an impression on Barnet who similarly aspired to be another link in the great tradition of the old masters admired by his teacher—Velasquez, Titian, Ingres, and David. (p. 9)

Barnet spoke to me on a couple of occasions about the importance to him of the neoclassical paintings of the French master Jean-Auguste-Dominique Ingres: "He was a big influence on my work." He seems to think frequently of the structure and forms in the paintings by artists of the great European painting tradition. He said:

> And that is what I admire in these artists. The feeling of weight of volume of putting things together, the form, so each piece to the other so that they're not just simply there and the spatial emptiness but with a structure underneath it. So I admire these people very much and they influenced me in my work and they occur over and over in my development.

Mentor to Others

"Oh yes, definitely! I had a lot of influence on different young artists at that time." Will Barnet, as in all his speaking to me, was very clear that he was "very much of a teacher too." His words harbored no hesitation or shame as some artists seem to have in teaching others what he knew and cared about in painting, drawing, printmaking, and the history of art, and how one can look at it.

His teaching, and thus mentoring, has spanned four decades at what is considered the most serious places of learning to be an artist in the United States: the Art Students League, The Cooper Union, and the Pennsylvania Academy of Art. Even at the age of 101, Mr. Barnet still saw himself teaching. When I told him how his discussion of the influence of the masters on him was "very helpful to me," he said, "Well, I want to be as helpful as I can to you because it was a very important part of my teaching."

Will Barnet said, "I was teaching classical training, analysis of the masters and the abstract aspects of their work." The classical training he received as a young man in Boston he then shared with the young men who became his students beginning in the 1930s, through World War II, and afterward into the 1970s. He brought his passion for studying the masters to the next generation and sought to bring to them also the understanding of "the contemporary moderns of that time coming out" (Figure 5.5).

Many of the young men—and they were primarily men during the first decades of his teaching—came to schools of higher learning through the G.I. Bill of Rights, which allowed veterans to attend college via financing from the U.S. government. This was an opportunity to learn in the academies after fighting in the fields and cities of war-torn Europe and in the oceans that joined the continents and kept them apart with the thick water of distance. Of his work with men who otherwise would likely not have entered the ivy walls of academia, he was clear about the benefits of the G.I. Bill: "It gave all the young men a chance to better themselves, to educate themselves."

Will Barnet's interest in the masters goes beyond the masters of old to the value of the masters where the craft of the practice is reborn in the work of the moderns. Of the young men coming from war to the art school, Barnet said:

> I was a mentor to them. I introduced them to abstract art, modern art, which they were interested in. There weren't many teachers at the League who were teaching modern art.

The values that one learns in studying the masters, in being a disciple to the masters, do not confine one to a single period of human endeavor. But the acquisition of those skills and ways of seeing and doing in the discipline of painting and drawing is seen in the portraits of Modigliani as well as in those of Ingres. Picasso embodies the quality of 15th-century Spain in 20th-century Paris.

Angela Churchill told me, "I think you'll have to ask the people. How am I suppose to know that?" when I asked her if others thought of her as a mentor. This answer became apparent when in the spring of 2012 there was an exhibition of the work of some 25 artists at New York University's 80west Galleries titled *NYU Venice: 1974–2011, Artists and Angiola Churchill*. I missed the

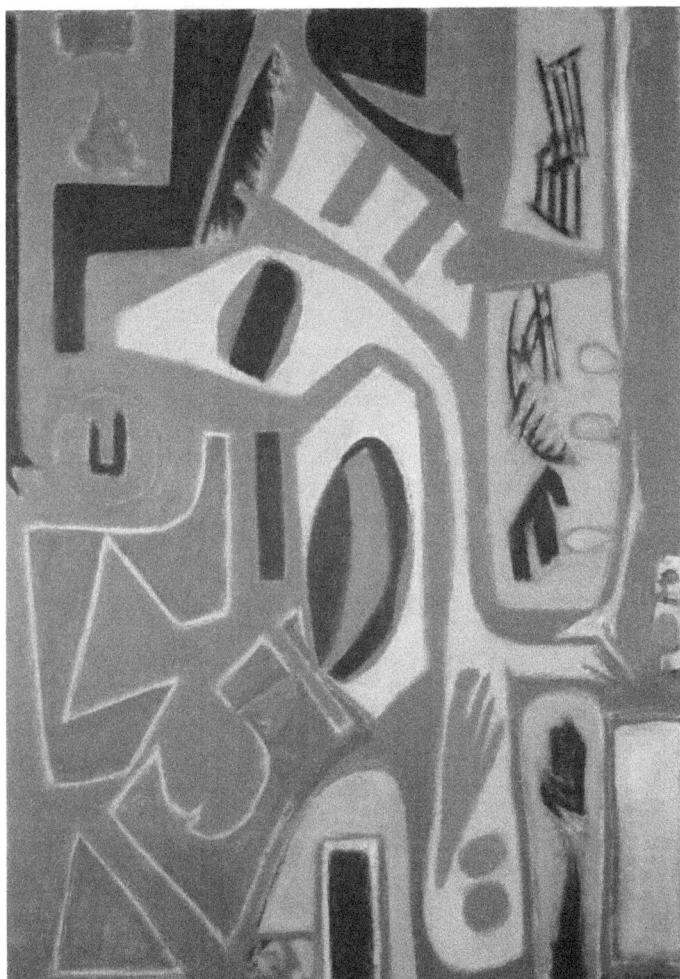

Figure 5.5 Will Barnet. *Creature*, 2007–08 (oil on canvas, 40 × 29 inches). Private Collection.

opening, but Angiola told me, "There must have been three hundred people there!" Though Angiola will not outright say that she has been a mentor to others, it has been apparent to me through people I have met who have been her students that she has very much been a mentor. The show and accompanying catalog give further support to the evidence of former students visiting her at home and speaking enthusiastically to me about her.

"We teachers are lucky. Our students are so good to us!" Angiola said to me by phone when telling me of the gala evening. I asked her what she meant. She elaborated, "With all our imperfections and everything, they still care about us, think of us, want to be around us." Angiola did add, "I have a lot of people that come and see me still and all of that. So I know something is hanging on." I do wonder if that is what it means to be of influence, that something hangs on after the time spent in the same physical place of classroom or studio as teacher and student. Does something happen where the student wants more and becomes a disciple, one who hangs on? When students keep coming back, are they renewing energies that were sparked during the time of shared teaching and learning? Are they seeking to stay in touch with a spark left inside (Figure 5.6)?

During our time speaking together, Angiola mentioned on a number of occasions the pull she felt between being an artist and being an educator, one responsible for teaching others, whether they are children at the Ethical Culture School or adults at New York University. She said to me, "I can't do it halfway. I can't not give myself to my students." Angiola gave herself to her students and they felt that giving. They have stayed in touch with her for decades.

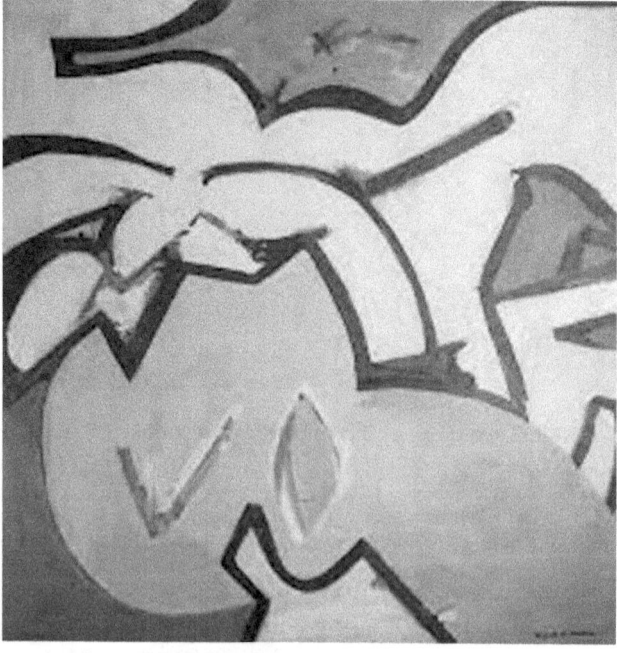

Figure 5.6 Angiola Churchill, untitled (painting, mixed media).

And so it is, so it seems, that in the teaching of others for reasons of earning a living or of social engagement or because of a passion to impart to others what one has learned and deemed of value, and so a desire to share gifts found and earned with others, one becomes a mentor. That seems to be part of the way here in the United States at the end of the 20th century and into the 21st. Regardless of the motivations for entering and staying in teaching, both Will Barnet and Angiola Churchill devoted great energies to their students through their teaching—not as a passing interest, but through decades and devotion.

Angiola said that while she was chair of the NYU art department and came into contact with so many of the art world's people—be they artists or curators or gallery owners, she did not feel "comfortable pushing myself" as an artist upon them. Her role in that institution was that of an educator and program administrator for the benefit of others, the students. In that capacity, "All my energies went into my teaching. I didn't have the same amount of energy to put into art."

Henry Finkelstein teaches painting at the Art Students League as Will Barnet did a few decades before. He also teaches at the National Academy School, both of which are in Manhattan. Of being a mentor to others, yes, he too has felt he has been. Regarding a group of young aspiring artists from Japan who took his classes at the National Academy, he said, "I did think of myself as a mentor. I stuck up for them. I tried to get them scholarship money."

Of the three artists in the study who have taught for a considerable part of their lives, Henry seems most suspect of the activity or vocation. He is also the only one of the artists whose parents were painters and teachers and is known as both. None of the other artists in this study had parents who were either painters or teachers. How much of Henry's conflict began in the home rather than in the classroom is all speculation, but it is within reason to speculate that his artist-teacher duality may come from a desire to define himself as separate from his parents. Or, equally possible, he saw from childhood the benefits and price of being both.

Henry felt—and this is consistent with his lack of desire to have disciples—that "It is very important to incite a kind of teaching where the student leaves. It's sad, but a good teacher becomes obsolete. That is a very important part of teaching." He does want his students to leave with "something to think about for the rest of your life." And this is what Henry felt Ruben Kadish and Nicholas Marsicano did for him: "as mine did" (Figure 5.7).

Henry is a painter. It is not a maybe thing for him; in fact, he never thought of doing anything else. Both his parents were painters and his role model from infancy, although not his mentors as one chooses mentors, and not parents, though parents are the first people we model ourselves on, our first teachers. No, his stated mentors were in fact—meaning artistic philosophical thought and pedagogical practice—very different from his parents' ways. His chosen mentors were more philosophical. Ruben Kadish, who began his artistic

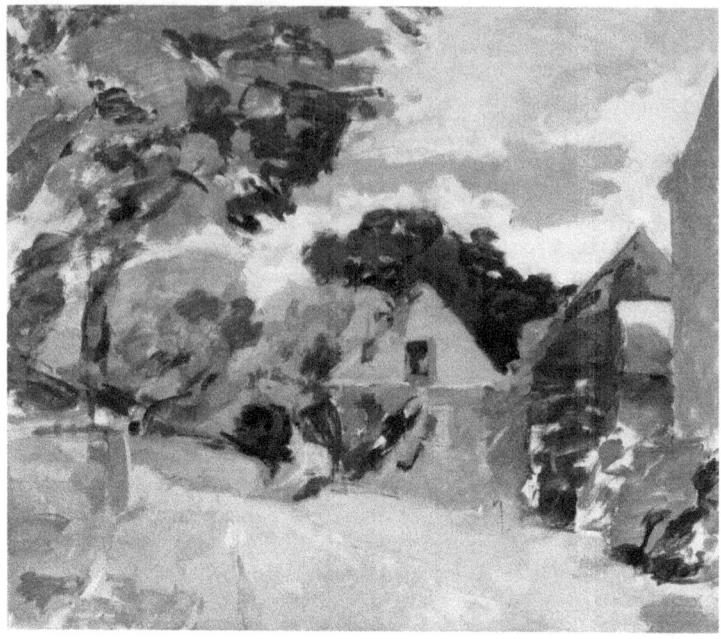

Figure 5.7 Henry Finkelstein. *Ruin by the Churchyard,* 2023 (oil on canvas, 45 × 50 inches).

endeavors as a painter with the comradeship of the painters Jackson Pollock and Philip Guston, came to be known as a sculptor, if anything, although Henry describes him as an "art philosopher." Moreover, Nicholas Marsicano painted not from observation as his parents did, but from other means—more memory and desire than perception.

Jarrod (Figure 5.8), the youngest of the four artists at the age of 35 at the time of this interview, has taught only minimally, yet he too considers himself to have been a mentor to interns at the Guggenheim Museum, where he worked in the exhibitions department for four years. He spoke of how he made an effort to relate to the interns who were younger than he in a way that expressed concern for their overall well-being and for their aspirations beyond the time they would spend at the Guggenheim. He said:

> because that job was based both in architecture and art, I felt like, there were definitely times when I was channeling Javier, when I would maybe talk to the interns about what they were doing, or about what they planned on doing, or what their future was, or on what they planned on doing within their education separate from the Guggenheim.

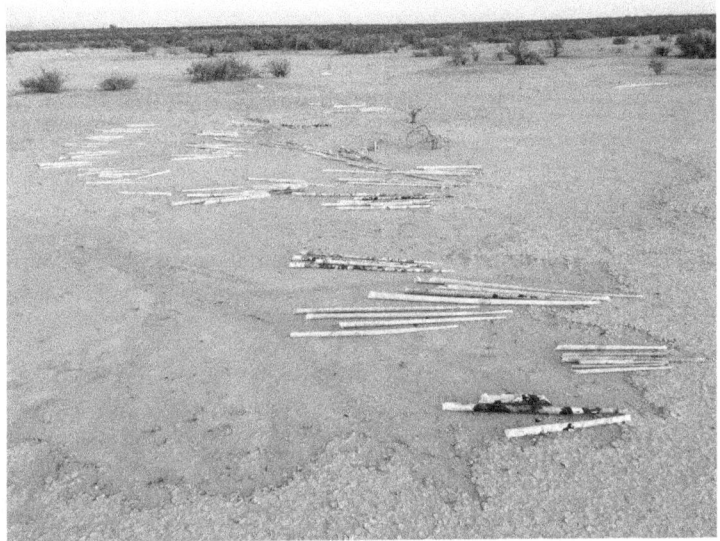

Figure 5.8 Jarrod Beck. *Disruption Regime* (Detail), 2010–present (Cast Plaster on 5 acres).

Permanent Installation outside Terlingua, TX, and Supported by Inde/Jacobs Gallery, Marfa, TX.

Teaching From Art

I spoke with Angiola on a number of visits. During one, with the formal interview long past, she spoke to me enthusiastically of the studio classes she taught while a professor of art education at NYU.

From my first conversations with Angiola, I got the impression that she stayed away from looking at others' art in her own art making and so in her teaching of art. This did not make much sense because way back in the year 2000, I remember her passion for the paintings of Arshile Gorky. When I mentioned his name, I recall her saying something like, "Oh Gorky! Now that's something else." From the tone in her voice, this meant to me that she was in awe of Gorky's paintings and that they were on a plane above so much of what is called art that it is a whole other thing to even consider mentioning them in the same breath.

This one day, Angiola told me about an advanced painting class that she taught, where she would project on the wall of the studio an image of a great painting from the past. One example was Géricault's *The Raft of the Medusa*. The task she gave her students was to draw the figures and forms out and then as a group paint it all in the two or three hours of the class. It was "an exhilarating experience! It gives you a sense of power, a sense of your own power and what you can do." Thus, when Angiola taught an advanced painting class, they spent much time working with past paintings in one way or another and all because the students were learning. As she said:

> Yeah, painted *The Raft of the Medusa* and all that. In the meantime, we were learning something, for God's sake. We stepped back and it also felt pretty good when the painting was up in two hours or when the painting class was over and we had painted that, a thing like that!

In another exercise, she would direct the students to look at actual paintings she had taken out of the collection of the university for the length of the class, saying to them:

> Pick something that you have a real affinity for. One of these guys. One of these four guys. These four guys, anything you have an affinity for. And paint a painting for the next three hours that is off of this painting.

Angiola said, "It seemed to me that that was the way to teach, to teach them to understand art," referring to her painting class in which the students made paintings based on looking at real paintings done by artists in the university's art collection. And so it is.

Will Barnet (Figure 5.9) spoke much about how he taught his students, many of them soldiers from the war, how to analyze the abstract element of a work of art, how to see the structure of it, whether it was a painting by Ingres from the 19th century or by Picasso from the 20th century.

Feelings About the Word "Disciple"

When I was speaking to Henry about his students and I asked him if he thought of himself "as a mentor and them as disciples," he told me he did not like the word "disciple." When I asked him, "What word would you use rather than 'disciple'?" he replied, "Students." He built on this saying that:

> Disciple to me implies that you presume the role of Jesus. And I would like to be inspirational, but you can get a little too grandiose teaching. And that's very unhealthy.

Henry's response to the term "disciple" is consistent with his feeling that "it's important to remain an artist first and a teacher second and not take yourself so seriously that you have disciples." At different moments in our interview, he made statements that gave the impression he did not so much trust the mentor and disciple relationship or teacher and student relationship to be without its perils.

Henry expressed concern for both the teacher becoming too grandiose and losing his priority to "remain an artist first" and for students who may become

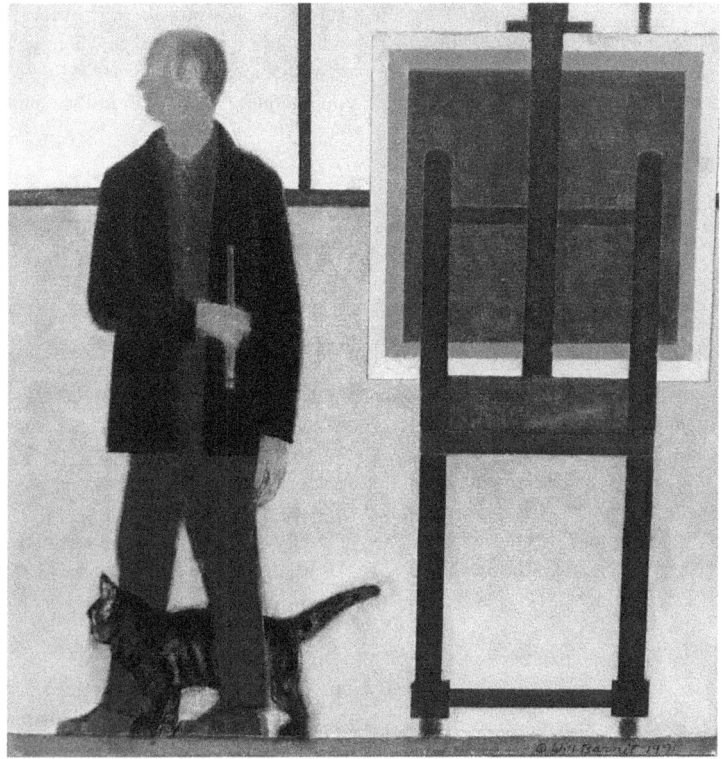

Figure 5.9 Will Barnet. *Self Portrait with Minou*, 1991 (oil on canvas, 29 1/4 × 28 1/2 inches).

© The Estate of Will Barnet, courtesy Alexandre Gallery, New York.

so in awe of a teacher that they never go out on their own and cease to grow. He said:

> It's very important to incite a kind of teaching where the student leaves. It's sad, but a good teacher becomes obsolete. That's a very important part of teaching.

Jarrod expressed no conflict with the word and its connotations. When I asked him if he had ever considered himself a disciple of someone, he said:

> I think when I was eighteen and a student of Javier's I got feeling like I was a disciple of his. I took a lot of his studios. I think other people saw me as a disciple of his.

Javier was his undergraduate architecture teacher at Tulane University. When I asked Jarrod, "Would you encourage future relationships where you would play the role as a mentor to someone or potentially as a disciple of someone?" he replied, "Yes. Yes, I would encourage that." He further built on this by saying:

> I would become a disciple again, I think. Although I feel like I've expanded beyond that kind of relationship with anybody. I do feel like I'm on a quest that may bring me into the orbit of someone else's power. And I would like to think I would be able to let go of, you know, of my own, of my own entity for a slight moment and become connected with this person. Let go of my own ego to be a disciple for somebody.

Although, like Henry, he did have some misgivings about becoming a mentor to someone and they being his disciple, Jarrod said:

> I think I've learned a lot from my mentors in ways, although I'm not perfect, I think I would definitely welcome someone who, a disciple. I think it's a dangerous, it can be, you have to really be all. If you're going to take the, be a mentor, I think you have to be very careful with another person's emotions.

Will Barnet expressed no reservations about the terms "mentor" or "disciple," though in our discussion, he never referred to his students as disciples. He freely used the term "mentor" to describe what the masters were to him and what he was to many a student. "I was a mentor to them" he said. And, "Oh yes, definitely. I had a lot of influence on different young artists at that time" was his response to my question if he had become a mentor to any of his students.

Mentor and Disciple Become Equals in Friendship

Will Barnet taught Robert Blackburn the art of lithography. Barnet said, "Bob loved lithography. He was passionate about it." Blackburn, whom I shall refer to as Bob because I worked in his printshop for two years on my work, was an apprentice to Barnet to whom he went to learn lithography at the Art Students League. Bob was black and racism toward people of African descent greatly prohibited their educational opportunities. Few were the master printmakers with whom Bob could study. Barnet seems to have cared for people regardless of skin color and cared about passing on the craft of lithography more than he did about societal norms of racial segregation.

The master printmaker Barnet and his disciple in lithography Blackburn became great friends for nearly 50 years. Barnet said of Bob, "So he played a big part in my life. And I played a big part in his life, you know. We were very good friends for years and years and years."

The Senior Curator at the Smithsonian American Art Museum, Joann Moser (2008), wrote:

> When he began to print lithographs with Robert Blackburn in 1951, he assumed the role of a master printer training an eager apprentice. At that time there were few opportunities for an artist to learn the craft of lithographic printing, especially for an African-American artist. After being rebuffed elsewhere, Blackburn found a willing and skilled teacher in Barnet, who worked with him until he became a master in his own right and established an important printmaking workshop. (p. ix)

Will Barnet mentioned other students who became "very close friends" after periods of studying with him. When I asked him if he had felt close to any mentors or students in his life, he said of past students:

> Well, yes. I can't remember some of the names because they've already gone. They've died. I lost so many since I outlived them. We were very close. We use to have parties. Somebody who was very close to me was Henry Pearson. We were very close friends. He studied with me at the League and we became very close, for years. And the other one was Arnold Singer, a very close friend. Even a number of others. I can't remember the names anymore. Names are difficult when you get older.

Jarrod Beck also spoke of how over time and greater and greater collaboration outside the classroom, he began to see his former mentor Margot as a friend and confidant as well. To the question "How do you think she saw you?" Jarrod replied,

> I wondered to this one point if she respected me, if she thought of me as an artist. I know that she thought of me as a very friendly polite, but also kind of crazy and fun student who was interesting and treated her with respect and treated her not as a professor, but as a friend. I was sincerely interested in her stories and in her life. I felt like maybe sometimes she thought of me as a confidant.

Jarrod describes how he and Margot came to be other than mentor and disciple, using the term "friendship" to describe how they related:

> A big thing that happened in our relationship, our friendship, was that when I finished grad school, I came…to teach at UT for the fall semester and at the very same time she had received a very large commission to do a public art piece in Houston. And she hired me to work with her to kind of figure out the project.

Other Commonalities That Arose

In this section, I discuss other themes that emerged from my discussions with the artists of the study who were not the main subjects of the study nor were the study's reason for being, yet they arose in the discussions and merit a presentation as data and, later, as areas to be discussed.

Essentially Growing Up Alone

From speaking with these four artists about their development as artist, I have come to find out that all of them essentially grew up as only children. This reminds me of a radio interview I once heard with the children's book author and illustrator Maurice Sendak, who explained that as a child he was very sickly and was forced to stay in the apartment while the other neighborhood children played outside. His many hours alone were less lonely because of the worlds he created through drawing. Drawing made alone time not so alone.

Will Barnet found himself in the Beverly Public Library of Massachusetts where the great masters of art history became his mentors. He was 10 years younger than his siblings and so "spent his childhood largely on his own" (Sheets, 2011, p. A22). His father came to Beverly from Russia and Will was born in Beverly.

Jarrod Beck told me that he too essentially grew up alone. He lived primarily with his mother and saw his father only for a day a couple of times a year when his mother and he would drive down to spend the afternoon or day with him. "So it was Mom and I from age 1-8," he wrote me. When his mother remarried, he then had a step-sister of about the same age whom he saw only every other weekend. About drawing, he said, "It was presented to me as something to do and I grew up alone and I read a lot and I drew."

Angiola also grew up as an only child, although when she was 12, her brother was born. She said:

> For one thing, I was an only child, so therefore, I had to create my world. Had to create a world in which I was operating. But, my mother said I was very happy there, and I closed her out, I closed everybody out. And I just did my thing, maybe except for a cat.

Henry too grew up like an only child. His sister is 12 years older and "she went away to college at the age of 16," leaving him alone with his parents from the age of 4 on for the most part.

Parental Influences

Will Barnet had no artists in his family. "They came from Europe. I don't know the location. But somewhere probably outside of, between, Russia and

Poland, areas like that, and Czechoslovakia." His father sought a better life in America like so many Europeans and found work in the factories of Beverly, Massachusetts, in the early 1900s. "He worked in a factory, Beverly Shoe Manufacturing. And he built machines for making shoes."

The extent of parental encouragement was that his father let him use the basement as a studio when he was in high school and did not impede his self-study. Of his father, Barnet said:

> He's a worker. A worker. But also, he was also a very sensitive man and he liked nature a lot and after work he would make a nice garden and grow plants and things like that. He was a mixture of a worker who later on after work would do something else in nature. That was my father.

He further explained to me that during World War I when he was young, "The people who were artists mainly came from the upper classes." Thus he explained to me why he did not receive familial encouragement to become an artist,

> My parents were not encouraging. My family was not encouraging. There was very little encouragement to be an artist in the first world war, in the twenties.

Angiola (Figure 5.10) received endless adoration from her mother with whom she primarily lived because her father remained in America when Angiola and her mother went to Italy upon doctors' recommendations when she was a sickly infant struggling for her life. Her parents were not artists. And while Angiola impressed upon me again and again that art was all around her in the town she grew up in near Milan, and that her aunt owned the only art store in town and she had all the materials she could want and more, what seemed most exciting were the teen boys who came to her aunt's store to buy the drawing materials and paper they needed for their after-school studies in drawing and architecture. Angiola did not have parental modeling in how to be an artist—not that being a fine artist was something people did, though certainly, people used drawing skills in the fine artisan work done for centuries upon centuries in the section of Italy where she grew up.

Henry (Figure 5.11) grew up with a painter mom and a painter dad, and both his parents taught painting and drawing in and around New York City at the college and graduate level. His life, as do all of ours, seems defined by parental influences. In his home in New York City, many artists visited his parents and one can imagine the daily conversations occurring throughout the day touching upon painting, drawing, being an artist, and the work of other artists, present and past.

Jarrod (Figure 5.12), though receiving much encouragement from his mother with whom he lived primarily and only rarely seeing his father, did not have a parental role model as an artist. He did take quickly to making art in elementary school where he gained the attention and admiration of teachers

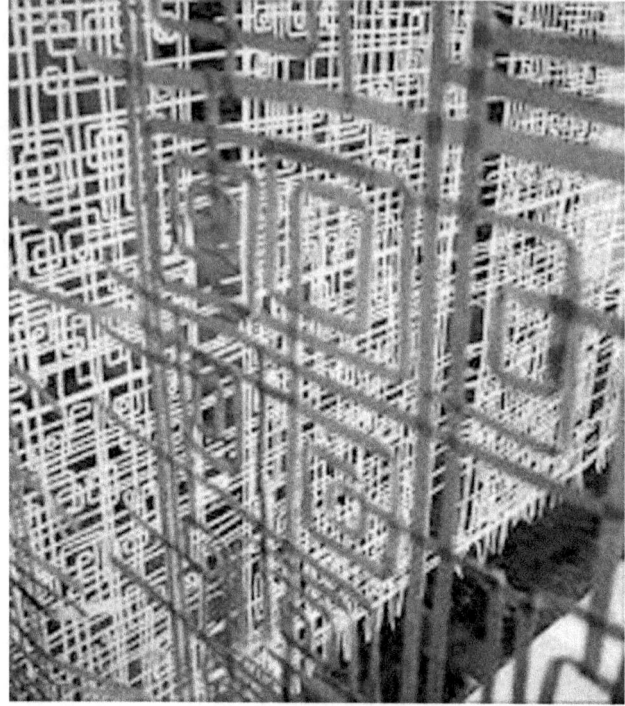

Figure 5.10 Angiola Churchill. *Oltre Il Giardino* (partial installation view), 2003.
The Museo Fortuny, Venice, Italy.

and experienced good feelings. As with most people, receiving good feelings prompts us to do more of the same that engendered us to receive those feelings in the first place.

Idleness

On this topic, Henry told me:

> I mean I had years of idleness. So did friends of mine. I wasn't the only one. It wasn't quite Bonnard's aloof idleness, but there wasn't this pressure to make something of yourself. There was this pressure to make something mean something to you!

Angiola mentioned idleness too—the time to do nothing, or more specifically, the time to not do something that demanded time and thought, other than

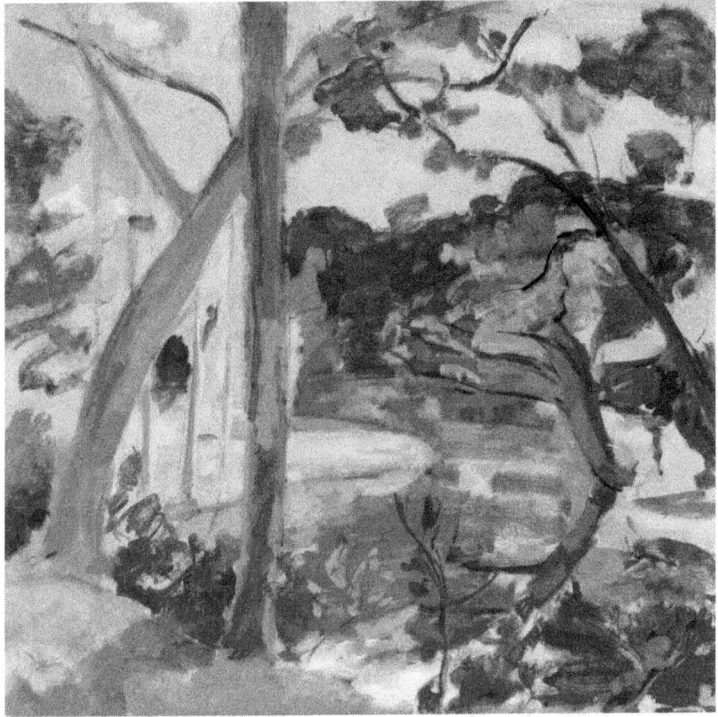

Figure 5.11 Henry Finkelstein. *Pond at Pommerit II*, 2023 (oil on canvas, 48 × 50).

going where the mind might wander in thinking of paintings and sculptures and passing the day.

Angiola remembered a time when she had just finished high school in New York City; the following year, she was not in a formal school but learned so much just from being in New York City where artists were and visiting the Whitney Museum which was then on 8th Street. "I hung around. I can tell you about all my hanging around with the Abstract Expressionists."

Angiola spoke of being a young woman of 18 years and visiting Hans Hofmann's school and how "Hofmann didn't mind. He was very nice." She spoke of how she was in the midst of what is now considered history in the movement of artists in New York that came to be known as the Abstract Expressionists. Her time was not idle in the sense of doing nothing, but it was open in that she did not have specific responsibilities beyond how she chose to spend her time that year. She studied the artists of Greenwich Village and went in and out of the school of Hans Hofmann.

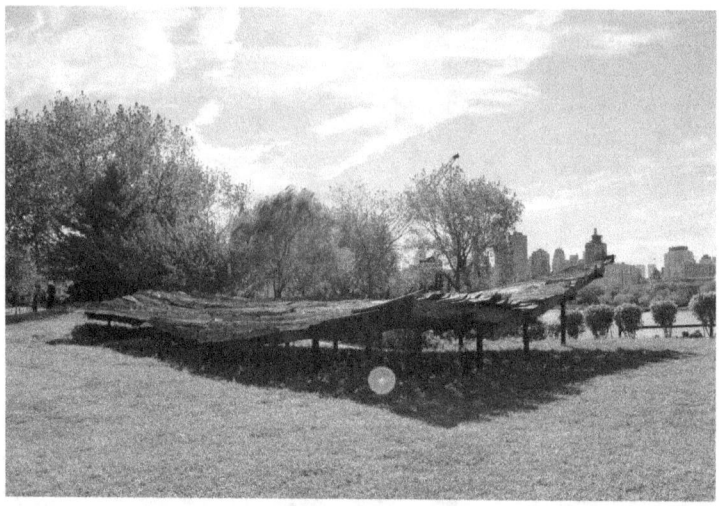

Figure 5.12 Jarrod Beck. *Quarry*, 2012–13 (installation).
Socrates Sculpture Park, Long Island City, NY.

Neither Will Barnet nor Jarrod Beck mentioned times of idleness when they did not work or attend school. Will Barnet was the father of three sons from his first marriage and had responsibility for providing for a family early in his life. Jarrod spent considerable time in graduate school and artists' residencies, which did allow for long periods when he could focus on his work, although he never described these as times when he had the freedom of doing whatever he chose. These seemed to be periods of focused work on art making.

The Art World

Will Barnet (Figure 5.13) told me that "The art world is a very strange place, you know" when he explained to me that while he, in part, made a living as a printer and had "done as much graphic work as any graphic man living during my time and afterward," he really wanted to be known as a painter. Painters had a higher place of value in the hierarchy of art: "I've been in the art world for eighty years, so." What can I say to that? Will Barnet had been in the art world longer than most people live.

"I use to go to The Club and listen to everything. I don't know what I was hearing or anything. But I was part of everything!" Angiola told me when I asked her about the influence of others she came into contact with while she wandered in and out of New York City's art places. She found herself in the

Figure 5.13 Will Barnet. *Eden*, 1964–65 (oil on canvas, 88 × 43 inches).

© *The Estate of Will Barnet, courtesy Alexandre Gallery, New York.*

midst of what would become the history of American art in the mid-20th century in books that speak of such things. She was living in New York City and hanging out at Hans Hofmann's School and around the famous or infamous 8th Street Club, where many founding members of the Abstract Expressionists— or as Dore Ashton (1973) prefers to call them, The New York School

artists—spent their time drinking, arguing, and discussing art and life as artists are wont to do. Whatever the name, Angiola did not like what she saw and
at that moment of being an 18-year-old young woman decided, "I didn't like
the art world."

> I was at 8th Street for a year. I decided, "Well, I can't go on like this!"
> I decided one thing, for one thing, I decided, I didn't like the art world.
> Because I saw the men were pigs! And I didn't like it. And I didn't want to
> become a victim of pigs!

She also explained that while Hans Hofmann "was very nice," she felt
his attention went all to the men and he seemed to think that women were
inherently weaker as painters. While Angiola understood there was not much
reason for Hofmann to pay much attention to her because, as she said, "I was
a kid, hanging around" and the "other people were more grown up and they
were paying too," she did recall having a not-right feeling when Hofmann
spoke about a woman's accomplishment by comparing it to a man's.

> And Hofmann paid so much attention to them and to the males that I…
> something happened that was in my mind. It didn't come to the fore. But
> it was in my mind that he used to say when a woman did something, he
> used to say, "That's pretty good for a woman! Look, a woman did this!"

Angiola (Figure 5.14) entered the world of teaching where she loved
working with the children at the Ethical Culture School and later taught in the
art department of New York University for nearly 40 years. All the while, she
made art but was far more involved in teaching others than in exhibiting and
selling works or trying to do those things.

Henry (Figure 5.15) made distinctions between making paintings in the
search for creating something of great value and to be a careerist. Though
Henry is very successful by most artists' standards in terms of his work, respect for his work, and sales, he is not considered a superstar in the art world,
and no longer and not for a while has a gallery in New York City represented
him although he was born, works, and lives in the city.

Henry lamented that he does not really know what is going on in today's
galleries, saying, "I don't go to shows a lot. I'm not very aware of my own
time. And I have some anxiety about that." He also felt badly that he could not
help a group of young foreign students whom he thought merited the showing
of their work.

> They're not American citizens. They're not allowed to work here or any-
> thing. I mean I guess if you want to get a gallery show, it's your responsi-
> bility to do it. But I don't even know how to do that myself.

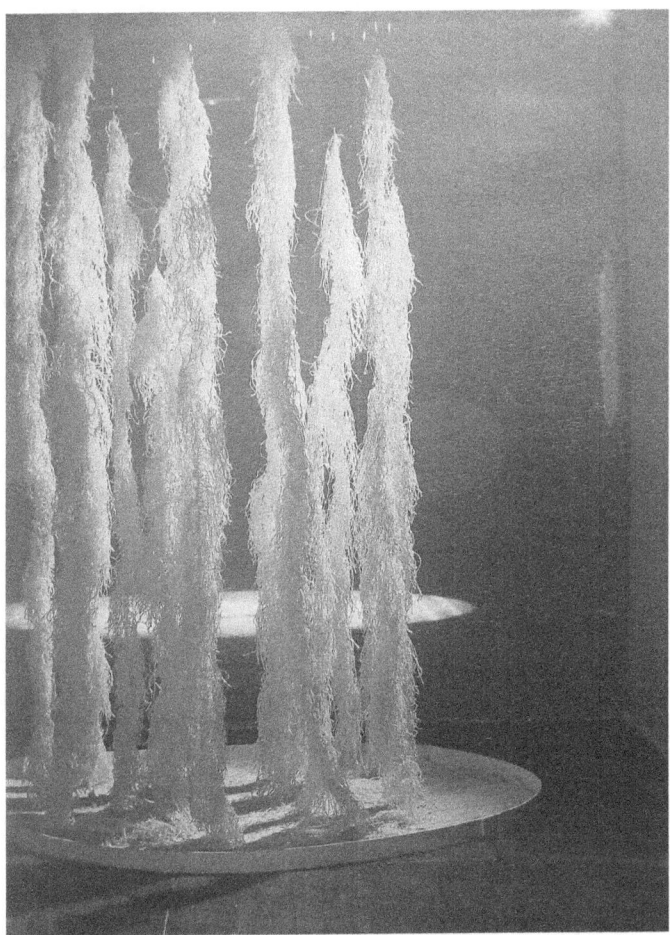

Figure 5.14 Angiola Churchill. *Oltre Il Giardino* (partial installation view), 2003.
The Museo Fortuny, Venice, Italy.

Yet, in going to hear a lecture with him about the artist Robert DeNiro Sr. by the art critic Martica Swain at the New York Studio School in the Spring of 2012, it became more obvious to me that Henry grew up if not in "the art world" of New York, than in "an art world" in New York. His parents knew Robert DeNiro Sr. and Martica Swain, it seems. She quoted Henry's father Louis Finkelstein in her lecture that evening. And after the lecture many an artist came up to Henry to renew acquaintances.

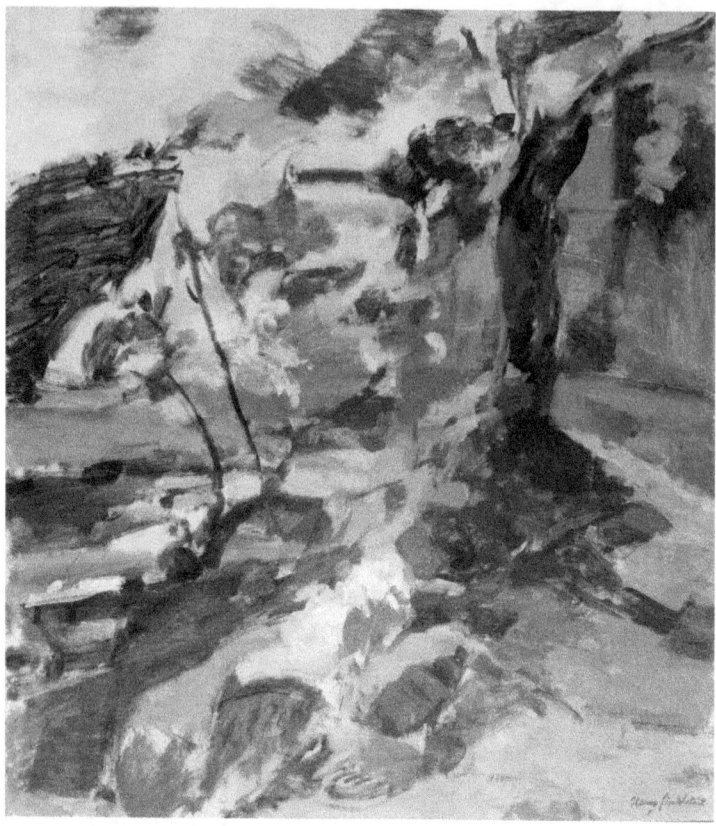

Figure 5.15 Henry Finkelstein. *The Mill at Pommerit,* 2023 (oil on canvas, 50 × 46 inches).

Though Jarrod (Figure 5.16) did not speak specifically about the art world as our conversation did not go there, he has had great success in it making work for with and at many an art institution. He continues a most prolific career using an extraordinary variety of materials and means.

Mentors in Our Minds

Mentors in our minds are those whom we chose to apprentice to yet whom we never met. They are role models for us from the discipline, historical figures. For me, Arshile Gorky became a mentor in my mind in that I would think about how it was that he became an artist and what he did as an artist and I would model my behavior on that. Picasso may have taken Velázquez as a

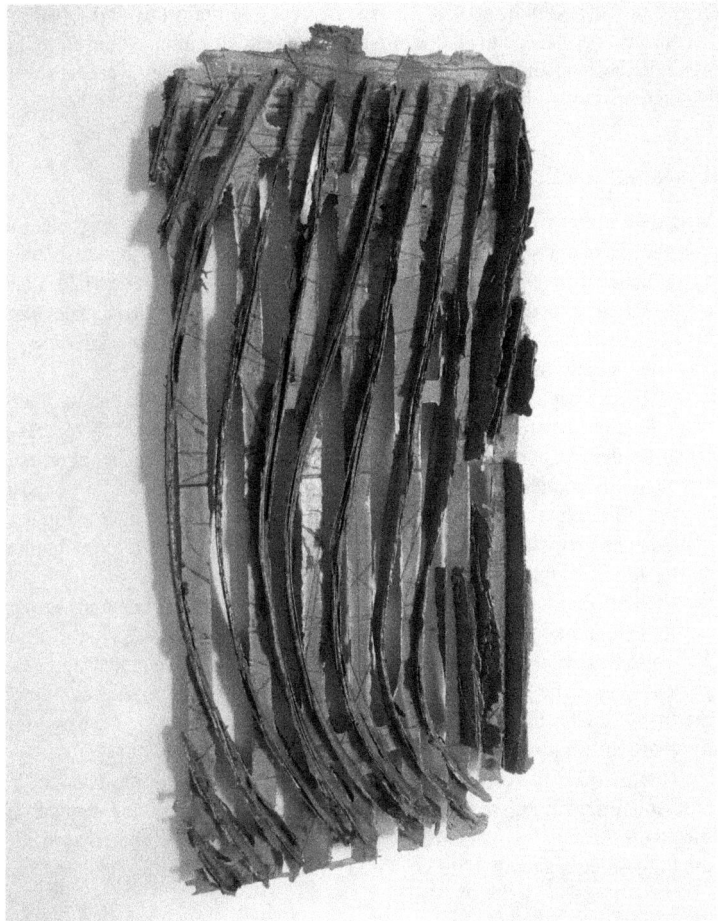

Figure 5.16 Jarrod Beck. *xfg*, 2019 (cast iron, 27 × 40 × 4).

historical mentor, a mentor in the mind, as one whose ways and work one seeks to learn from to become like.

Will Barnet chose the masters of the art of painting to be his mentors. He found great insights and inspiration in the work of Ingres and Daumier. As he told me, "Let's just say the masters were my mentors." During his 80-year career, the masters were always by his side, including the masters of the Native American arts.

I call these mentors from history that we turn to as mentors in our minds for that is where we find them, in our thoughts. We chose to disciple ourselves to one in the discipline whom we saw as great in an effort to find a path to becoming an artist. Arshile Gorky first followed and disciplined himself to the work of Cezanne and then Picasso (Schwabacher, 1957), they were in a way his mentors though he never met them.

Teaching as a Practice of Human Nurturance

When we teach, we teach people. We also teach the elements, concepts, or information of a discipline or field of study. Here, I want to talk about teaching as a practice of instructing and guiding others, usually younger people. I am asking that we recognize the deep affections and connections that can develop between teacher and student and consider this not just the transmission of information, but the nurturance of the human spirit.

All people need to be nurtured and cared for and we provide that to others and others provide that to us. It is a human need and behavior. Teaching is a human endeavor, person to person even if it is one person to many at a time. Through this human endeavor, we reveal ourselves and come to know those we seek to teach, guide, and mentor. It is through this human interaction that connections between two are made and these connections nurture the human spirit, sustain it, and encourage it.

The transmission of information is valuable, but the whole human craves nurturance and sometimes this comes in the form of a teacher or mentor, someone who happens to care, does care. This caring is not lost upon the student. Nor is the student's need lost upon the teacher. A teacher can touch the lives of many and many touch his soul as well. In giving we are cared for. In caring for we give.

There is also the caring for and nurturing of the discipline. It could be mathematics, painting, dance, or writing. But it is that dual caring, that caring for others through the transmission of the values of the discipline that makes the biggest impact upon a life.

References

Ashton, D. (1973). *The New York School: A cultural reckoning.* New York, NY: Viking.
Moser, J. (2008). *Will Barnet: Catalogue raisonne 1931–2005: Etchings, lithographs, woodcuts, serigraphs.* New York, NY: John Szoke Editions.
Sheets, H. M. (2011). Staying power: The many forms of Will Barnet. *The New York Times,* October 9, p. AR22.
Schwabacher, E. K. (1957). *Arshile Gorky.* New York, NY: Macmillian.
Stavitsky, G. (2000). *Will Barnet: A timeless world.* Montclair, NJ: The Montclair Art Museum.

Index